YAHUAH
(יהוה)
RESTORATION GUIDE

YAHUAH
(יהוה)
RESTORATION GUIDE

Yeral E. Ogando

Christian Translation LLC
Printed in the USA.UU
2024

ISBN 13: 978-1-946249-97-5

DEDICATION:

This book is dedicated to the one and only lasting person who has always been there for me, no matter how stubborn I am:
YAHUAH

I also want to dedicate this work to you (the readers), because you have taken the time to read this Bible manual; I hope YAHUAH's blessing will be with each of you as you read this manual. And in a very special way, I want to dedicate this guide to the person who led me to create it, Hiraida Ogando Diaz

You all have a special place in my heart.
Always.

ACKNOWLEDGEMENTS:

I thank YAHUAH for allowing this guidance to come true and for giving me strength, wisdom and understanding to write it.

Special thanks to Hiraida Ogando Díaz, who has been the inspiration for making this guide a reality in our lives.

This has been a very blessed journey for my family, and the reward is worthy. Thanks to my children, *Bennett, Ethan* and *Nathan* for staying by my side through this journey. They know I love them.

YAHUAH
RESTORATION GUIDE

—⟨⟩⟨◇⟩⟨⟩—

Prayer

M y YAHUAH ELOHIYM I come before your presence in the name of your Beloved Son YAHUSHA, interceding and praying for every person who is reading this guide and who will continue to read it in the course of the years to come.

Give them understanding and wisdom so that they can read this guide with an opened mind and a heart completely willing to receive the truth of your word. Touch their hearts and open their eyes so that the light of your truth becomes a reality in each one of them. In the mighty name of YAHUSHA. Amen.

∽

Contents

CHAPTER IV

CHAPTER V

CHAPTER VI

CHAPTER VII

CHAPTER VIII

CHAPTER IX

Executioners and Persecutors of the followers of YAHUAH 133

CHAPTER X

Salvation... 145

Conclusion

Prayer

Biography

Bibliography

INTRODUCTION

———◆———

I am pleased to share with each of you, my dear readers, what I believe will help you bring peace and tranquility to your lives and hearts, as well as joy. In this short guide we will find a lot of important information and we will restore the name of our Creator **YAHUAH** and of our Savior **YAHUSHA**.

Likewise, we will learn the true meaning of the names that humanity has been using to refer to our Creator and Savior and, in the same way, we will learn the truth behind His name to achieve freedom and enjoyment.

Most of us have been taught little about the **Feasts of YAHUAH** or **Biblical Feasts.** In fact, we have even been led to believe that these feasts have been abolished and that we no longer need to celebrate them in our lives. However, we are induced from childhood to celebrate every pagan holiday ever and ever, including all holidays in veneration of a pagan

1

person, deity or gods.

Then we come to a small crossroads that makes us think about what is truly convenient or profitable for us as children of the Creator **YAHUAH**. However, this will be a decision that each of us will have to make on our own.

We will encounter not only challenging and perhaps even surprising and shocking concepts for some, but the fact is that the meaning of many of them is contrary to what we have been told or taught. Just as the Apostle Paul, when in *1 Thessalonians 5: 21 he tells us,* Prove all things; hold fast that which is good. *H*e commands you to examine or scrutinize everything and, even more, to retain the good, I urge you to make your own researches for information on the topics discussed here. Because this is what will lead us to a pleasant life and in obedience to our Creator **YAHUAH** and Savior **YAHUSHA**.

In this study we will know the true names of our Creator **YAHUAH** and the true name of our Savior **YAHUSHA** and the reason for its importance; we will learn about the Hebrew Alphabet, the different calendars and their relevance in our lives. Likewise, we will see the origin of demons, the slavery of YAHUAH's people, the commandments and some terms such as ELOHIYM, lord, Jesus and Christ, among others, taking into account the background and history of the Roman Emperor Constantine. Finally, we will learn some facts about the early versions of the Bible and the Biblical Feasts of **YAHUAH**.

I pray to my **YAHUAH ELOHIYM** that He may give

wisdom and understanding to every person who has the opportunity to read and share this information in the name of His beloved Son **YAHUSHA**. We must remember that in no way the presentation of the data presented here is intended to criticize or debate, much less denigrate anyone. The only goal is that we know the truth, and that we can finally be free and put our trust in **YAHUAH**.

CHAPTER I

THE CREATION

We all know the story of creation and how **YAHUAH** created everything in six days and on the seventh day he rested. Let's then look at a slightly broader perspective on creation and what things were created on every day.

Day one Jubilees 2:2 - Berēshīṯh 1:1-5	Day two Jubilees 2:4 - Berēshīṯh 1:6-8	Day three Jubilees 2:5-7 - Berēshīṯh 1:9-13
The heavens The waters Angels The Spirits Abyss Darkness Light	Firmament	Bodies of Water The dew Plants The Garden of Eden

Day four Jubilees 2:8-10 - Berēshīth 1:14-19	Day five Jubilees 2:11-12 - Berēshīth 1:20-23	Day six Jubilees 2:13-14 - Berēshīth 1:24-31
The Sun The Moon The Stars	Sea Monsters Marine Life The Birds	Terrestrial Animals Cattle Everything that moves on earth The Man
Day seven **Jubilees 2:17-18 - Berēshīth 2:1-3**		
Jubilees 2: 17-18. And he gave us a great sign, the Shabbath day, that we should work six days, but keep the Shabbath on the seventh day of all work. 18. And all the angels of the presence, and all the angels of sanctification, these two great classes: He has hidden us to keep the Shabbath with Him in heaven and on earth.		

These are the twenty-two works of creation and the greatest wonder created by **YAHUAH** since the beginning of mankind: the seventh day as a rest, which should be kept both on earth and in heaven.

Day 1: YAHUAH created the heavens, the waters, the angels (all kinds of angels), the spirits (meaning every living spirit, including that of man), the abysses, darkness (nocturnal part of nature) and light (daytime part of nature). It is important to remember that the light we are talking about here is not sunlight.

Day 2: YAHUAH only created the firmament on

the second day. That is, the solid vault of heaven or celestial vault that can be seen from any point on Earth. That's where we can see the clouds moving, the birds flying, the sun, the moon and the stars.

Day 3: YAHUAH created the bodies of water (**YAHUAH** ordered the waters to be grouped in a single place or body of water), the dew, all the plants and the Garden of Eden.

Day 4: YAHUAH created the sun, the moon and the stars. Only on the fourth day were these stars or lights created, not before. And they were placed in the firmament to divide the light from the darkness, to rule over the day and the night. On the fourth day, we no longer depend only on the light and darkness of nature, but now we have the lights created for day and night.

Day 5: YAHUAH created the sea monsters, all the marine or aquatic life and all kinds of birds. Although we have not seen them, sea monsters exist or existed.

Day 6: YAHUAH created all the animals on the face of the earth, all kinds of livestock, everything that moves on earth and finally, **YAHUAH** created man. Although it may seem surprising, on the sixth day **YAHUAH** created the shell or body of man (formed from the dust of the earth) and then breathed the breath of life or spirit (ruach) created on the first day.

Day 7: YAHUAH created the Shabbath to be kept both on earth and in the heavens.

Everything **YAHUAH** created was good and took pleasure in all his creation. There was absolutely nothing wrong or evil-inclined. **YAHUAH** has no ties to evil or the creation of evil. There is no evil in His creation and evil was NOT created by **YAHUAH**.

The Garden of Eden and the Fall

Creation has been completed and rest happens on the seventh day. The Garden of Eden was created on the third day for the enjoyment and delight of the protagonists of creation (Âdâm and Chawwâh).

Berēshîṯh 2:¹⁵⁻¹⁷ *And **YAHUAH ĔLÔHÎYM** took Âdâm, and put him into the Garden of Eden to dress it and to keep it. ¹⁶ And **YAHUAH ĔLÔHÎYM** commanded Âdâm, saying, Of every tree of the garden you may freely eat: ¹⁷ But of the tree of the knowledge of good and evil, you shall not eat of it: for in the day that you eat thereof you shall surely die.*

The man had the responsibility to till and keep the garden. Everything that was in the garden was for the enjoyment and delight of man, however, there was only one prohibition or rule: the man should not eat from the tree of the *knowledge of good and evil*.

The man knew only the good, and that everything came from **YAHUAH** however, by tasting the tree of the knowledge of good and EVIL, their eyes were opened and they began to recognize or know the difference between good and evil.

Therefore, by disobeying YAHUAH's command, Âdâm and Chawwâh would bear the consequences of their actions as **YAHUAH** had already ordered, *"For in the day that you eat of it, you will surely die."* And so it was, the very day they ate they died. That has been the norm since the fall until the end of time where every human being born of sin dies the same day of his birth.

For **YAHUAH** *a day is like a thousand years and a thousand years like a day.* That is why no human being has reached a thousand years or a full day on this earth. **Romans 3:** [23] *for all have sinned, and come short of the glory of* **ELOHIYM**. This is our reality and the result of sin or the fall. We are all born in sin and far from our Creator **YAHUAH**. The first sin is disobedience. That is why we are all born in disobedience to **YAHUAH** and to our parents.

Man is cast out of the Garden of Eden, and the woman, the Nâchâsh (not a serpent, but an angel), and the earth are cursed as a result of sin. That care that **YAHUAH** had with his creation (Âdâm and Chawwâh), that communion and communication, everything was affected and, as a result, the origin of evil began with sin or the fall.

It is from here that Qayin commits the first murder in the history of mankind. **YAHUAH** accepted Hebel's offering or the first fruits of its fruits and rejected Qayin's offering.

Qayin kills Hebel, marries his sister Awan and she gave birth to Chănôk. It is at this time that houses begin to be built on earth, and Qayin built the first city of the world with the name of his son. Chawwâh conceives and gives birth to Shêth who marries his sister Azura who gave birth to Ĕnôsh, who was the first to invoke the name of **YAHUAH** on earth. **Berēshīṯh 4:25 / Jubilees 4:12**.

Several generations later, Malaleel marries Dinah,

both of Shêth's offspring, and they have Îyrâd. In this year is that **YAHUAH** he sends his angels called Watchers to earth to teach mankind to make laws and justice on earth.

Jubilees 4: [15]... *Malaleel took Dinah, the daughter of Barachiel, his cousin, to be his wife. And she bare him a son in the third day of seven, in the sixth year, and he called his name Îyrâd (Jared): for in his days the angels came down from* **YAHUAH** *to the earth, the so-called "watchers", to teach the human race to make laws and justice on earth.*

And the son of Îyrâd, Chănôk is the first human being to learn scriptures and letters. **Jubilees 4**: [17-19] *This was the first of the human race born on earth who learned scripture, doctrine and wisdom, and wrote in a book the signs of heaven, according to the order of their months, so that men might know the seasons of the years, according to their order, by their months.* [18] *He was the first who wrote a revelation and bore witness to mankind in the earthly lineage. He narrated the centenary jubilees, he made known the days of the years, he established the months, and he told the weeks of the years, as we showed him.* [19] *He saw in a vision by night, in a dream, what has happened and what will happen, and what will happen to mankind in their generations until the Day of Judgment. He saw and knew everything, and wrote his testimony, leaving it as such on earth for all mankind and their generations.*

Incredibly the books of Chănôk were rejected and not included in the canon of the Bible. Even today many are still lost and do not read or scrutinize the writings of the first man to have received the revelations from the beginning of mankind until the Day of Judgment. His writings are in the so called Apocrypha, but people still don't know that Apocrypha simply means "hidden or secretly hidden". These treasures are still HIDDEN from humankind, because they don't want us to know the truth and be free.

Origin of the Demons

To begin with, let's go back a little to the beginning of civilization to be able to understand this topic, since we have been educated with false information for years. We always hear wrong phrases like, *Why did YAHUAH ELOHIYM create the demons?* Many have too many explanations to be able to justify such a false belief, one that has been eating away or d devouring the lives of many in our century.

However, the ancients did not suffer from these evils thoughts or these hallucinations as they do today. Before coming to an answer to this question, let's search the scriptures a little in order to arrive at the answer that so many have sought and apparently never found or simply turned a blind eye to the truth.

Let's go back to **Berēshīṯh 6:** *¹And it came to pass, when men began to multiply upon the face of the earth, and daughters were born unto them, ² that seeing **the children of ELOHIYM** that **the daughters of men** they were beautiful, they took for themselves women, choosing among all. ³ And **YAHUAH** said, my ruach (spirit) shall not contend with man forever, for verily he is flesh; but his days shall be an hundred and twenty years. ⁴ There were Nephîyl (giants) on the earth in those days, and also after they came **the children of ELOHIYM** at **the***

daughters of men, <u>and they bore them children</u>. *These were the valiant ones who from ancient times were men of renown.*

If we read the context of that chapter, we will understand that it is about the wickedness of men and the beginning of the construction of the ark as a consequence of said wickedness.

The children of ELOHIYM: they are the "children of <u>ELOHIYM</u>". There are several theories to try to define this term "children of ELOHIYM". The term Elohiym is the literal or correct translation of the word "ELOHIYM" in our language and we cannot say that it refers to the children or offspring of any human being. I think the Hebrew term is clear enough for us and that's why we can understand that these "sons of ELOHIYM" were angels and not humans.

We are going to read the same passage, but in the book of Jubilees 5: [1] *And it came to pass, when the sons of men began to multiply upon the face of the earth, and daughters were born unto them, the* **angels of ELOHIYM** *they saw them in a certain year of this jubilee, that they were beautiful to the sight; and they married all whom they chose, and bore them children, and they were* Nephîyl *(giants).*

That's how it all happened. At the beginning of humanity and after the Fall of man, **YAHUAH** sent the Watchers or angels to show the ways of **YAHUAH** to mankind and instruct them in the truth of their Creator. **Jubilees 4**: [15] *... for in his <u>(days of Jared)</u> days the angels of **YAHUAH** descended upon the earth, those who are called the **Watchers**, to instruct the children of men, and to do judgment* *and righteousness in the earth.*

Remember what **YAHUSHA** said, in heaven the angels neither marry nor are given in marriage. **Matthew 22:** *[30] For in the resurrection they will neither marry nor be given in marriage, but will be like the angels of **YAHUAH** in the sky.* In other words, angels do not experience the sexual desires that humans have.

However, when the **Watchers** were sent to minister to humanity, they took human corporeal form; this also included human needs, if they so choose. In the process of teaching and guiding humanity, the **Watchers** (angels), as they dwelt on earth with humans, they saw the beautiful daughters of men **"Berēshith 6**: *[1-4]"*and they joined them or better explained, they have sexual intercourse with them.

It is key that this concept is well understood since, by joining the daughters of men, they created a new race or species, one that was not part of the creation of **YAHUAH** but rather it was the creation of humans with the angels who broke the covenant with **YAHUAH**. The children of this union were called Nephilim in the Bible and were the giants of antiquity; in other words the Nephîyl. Again, they were not created by **YAHUAH**, were a PROCREATION or the product of the union of the Watchers with the daughters of men.

This new race then represents the absolute corruption of the creation or work of our Creator. For the first time in human history, the Watchers and the daughters of men had manipulated the DNA of the creation of **YAHUAH** and they had corrupted its creation with unclean blood. Their multiplication was gigantic, so that the whole creation was corrupted with this race that was not part of the creation of **YAHUAH**.

Jubilees 4: [22] *And he testified to the Watchers, that they had sinned with the daughters of men, for these had begun to unite, in order to defile themselves, with the daughters of men, and Chănôk testified against (them) all.*

Berēshīṯh 6: [5] *and ĔLÔHÎYM saw that the wickedness of man was great in the earth, and that every imagination of the thoughts of his heart was only evil continually.* This is the degree to which the contamination of creation reached because of the impurity of the new race of the Nephilim, so that **YAHUAH** decreed the flood to SAVE the only thing that was still pure of his creation. That is why Nôach found grace in the eyes of **YAHUAH. Berēshīṯh 6:** [9...] *Nôach was a **just** man and **perfect** in his generations, and Nôach walked with ĔLÔHÎYM.*

The term that the Hebrew uses to describe Nôach as perfect is "tâmıym (תָּמִים)" which means **Pure, without blemish, without fault**. In other words, Nôach was the only pure thing left of the creation of **YAHUAH**, so he sent the flood and all mankind perished. However, he was able to SAVE the pure part of his creation: Nôach with his wife and his three sons with their respective wives (8 people in total). The flood came by the defilement of the fallen angels with the daughters of men. As a result of the corruption of humanity, animals and the entire creation, YAHUAH decides to SAVE Nôach and his family and start over again.

Let us remember something crucial from this event. It happened approximately 7 generations after Adam and it happened in the times of Îyrâd (Jared). No angel nor women joined in sexual intercourse before that. Then **YAHUAH** sends the flood to purge humankind and SAVE the 8 people that were pure or whatever was left of his creation.

Although we all know this story and so far we are doing well, the part that most do not take into account is that ***the Nephilim perished in the flood, that evil or corrupted offspring was wiped out from his creation***, but since they were not part of the creation of **YAHUAH**, there was no place created for their spirits or souls. These are the ones we know as demons. In other words, the souls (spirits) of the Nephilim is what we know as Demons.

Origin of the Demons: *Children of the watchers (angels) and women; those who perished or died at the time of the flood. Those souls or spirits are the demons.*

Before that time, there was NOT a demon on earth or anywhere else, because they did not exist. The earth enjoyed nearly 400 to 700 years without demons.

As we can see, **YAHUAH** has never created anything that is evil, everything He created was good. Those who created the demons or demonic beings, whatever you want to call them, were the watchers (angels) and the men or daughters of men.

The mothers of these evil beings or demons perished, and the fathers, the watchers, were locked up in eternal prisons awaiting the day of the great judgment where they will receive total annihilation as retribution for their sin.

This means that demons do not have the power that most people attribute to them; they cannot touch you nor do any harm to you directly. They are incorporeal and to possess a human being, that person has to give the demon room and entry, in the very same way when they asked permission to **YAHUSHA** to enter the herd of pigs. Demons can only influence or use another weak human being to physically harm someone, but THEY CANNOT touch you.

It is at the moment when **YAHUAH** is ready to lock up all the demons that were procreated by the angels and humans that Mastema asks to **YAHUAH** let him keep some demons to fulfill his purpose on earth. **YAHUAH** grants his wish and leaves 10% of the demons obeying the voice and command of Mastema.

Normally we would think that the end of the race of the Nephilim and the Watchers was the flood, however, it is very sad to say that it was not so. There is a story in the book of Enki, an occult book, about a Nephilim demon that survived the flood and that continued very slowly and through the centuries with the bloodline of the Nephilim race, giants.

The most interesting or sad thing is that the doctrine of the Watchers has remained in active through the years. The pioneer or father of this doctrine is one of the descendants of Shem. **Jubilees 8**: *[1-4] In the twenty-ninth jubilee in the first week, in its beginning Arpakshad took a wife and her name was Rasueya, daughter of Susan, daughter of Elam, as a wife. And she bore him a son in the third year that week, and he called him **Qayinan**, 2 and the child grew up. And* *his father taught him to write. And he went out to find a place to build a city. 3 And he found a writing that the ancestors had engraved in stone. And he read what was in it. And he transcribed it. And he sinned because of what was in him, since there was in him the teaching of the Watchers by which they used to observe the omens of the sun and the moon and the stars within all the signs of heaven. 4 And he copied it, but he didn't say it because he was afraid to tell Arpakshad so that he wouldn't get angry with him about it.* Qayinan knew that it was a false or pagan doctrine, so it was forbidden by YAHUAH, that's why he kept it secret and did not inform his father *Arpakshad*. He copied these doctrines from the watchers and they have survived to this day. It is so much so that even in the churches themselves you can find the teachings and doctrines of the watchers.

The Tower of Babel

Many of us have heard about the Tower of Babel, but few of us stop to think about what really happened at that moment. **Berēshīth 11**: *² At that time there was only one language spoken in the whole earth.* This indicates to us that at that time people were still speaking the language of creation; a single language or tongue existed in humanity up to that point.

Jubilees 12: ²⁶ *And I opened his mouth and his ears and his lips and began to speak to him in Hebrew, in the language of creation.* In other words, Hebrew is the original language and was the language of creation, not the Modern Hebrew we know today, rather the ancient Hebrew.

Berēshīth 11: ⁴ *Then they said, Go to, let us build us* *a city and a tower, whose top may reach unto heaven; and let us **make us a name**, **lest we be scattered abroad** upon the face of the whole earth».* They all joined at unison in order to be famous and, more importantly, not to be scattered all over the earth.

They already knew that they would be scattered, but they were full of pride and arrogance, and they wanted to get to heaven. That is, to reach the firmament. **Jubilees 10**: [18] *"Behold, the sons of man have become wicked with wicked counsels, so that they are building a city and a tower for themselves in the land of Shinar."*

Let's understand the line of thinking here. Humanity had gone through the flood, from where the demons came out as a result of the union of the human being and the angels. Humanity is once again corrupting its ways. *"With perverse advice"*, that is, they were listening to evil voices or influences of the spirits of perdition or demons and learning from the doctrine of the Nephilim or the watchers.

To stop them from achieving their purposes, **YAHUAH ELOHIYM** decided to confuse the language they spoke, so he scattered them all over the face of the earth and, because of sin, the origin of all the languages of the earth were originated. That same Nephilim or demonic influence is the one that has been filling the heart and mind of humanity, which remains in force to this day.

Sedôm and Ămôrâh

It is after the flood and the confusion of tongues or languages that we come to the destruction of Sedôm and Ămôrâh. Many of us do not understand this biblical account because we have not been taught the truth of the scriptures, but let's look at it briefly.

Everyone remembers Abrâhâm, who had a nephew named Lôṭ. Their wealth and possessions had increased so much that they had to divide and live in separate places, and then Lôṭ stayed to live in the territories of Sedôm and Ămôrâh. You can read **Berēshiṯh 19** for better understanding.

The sin was so great in Sedôm and Ămôrâh that **YAHUAH** decreed that these cities be destroyed. Many people think it was because of homosexuality or lesbianism, but it's not like that. These are sins like all the others. The sin that overflowed the cup is in the following account.

Berēshiṯh 19: *[1 & 5] And there came **two angels** to Sedôm at even; and Lôṭ sat in the gate of Sedôm: and Lôṭ seeing them rose up to meet them; and he bowed himself with his face toward the ground. [5] And they called out unto Lôṭ, and said unto him, where are the men which came in to you this night? Bring them out unto us, **that we may know them**.*

Let me explain the key words in this verse, the same one that leads to the destruction of the inhabitants of this city, who wanted Lôṭ to deliver the visitors to them. *First they all knew that these two men were two angels and secondly* "so that **we may know them**". This term is used in scripture to refer to the moment when a man gets close to or knows a woman intimately, that is, and in clearer terms, when they have sexual intercourse.

This was the goal of the inhabitants of the city. Lôṭ

proposed to give them his two virgin daughters, but they refused because they were looking for something else. ¿Can you imagine what they were looking for?

The inhabitants of these cities had knowledge of the race of Nephilim who had been created at the time of the flood, and as they already had mixture of Nephilim blood, they sought to recreate or procreate again the same corruption that the Watchers had created in the past. Their goal was to create a new race again: union of humans with angels.

Therefore, they already knew that these men were divine and sought to return the procreation of their parents. But **YAHUAH** could not allow such corruption to happen once again with His creation, and then He decreed the destruction of Sedôm and Ămôrâh with fire from heaven.

Sadly, the world is already like Sedôm and Ămôrâh and the accompanying imminent judgment of destruction is near. The human being is modifying the DNA and corrupting the creation of **YAHUAH** in a great way, and this that you call evolution or development will become the destruction of humanity once again and for the last time.

∽

CHAPTER II

YÔSÊPH (JOSEPH) AND SLAVERY

Remember Yaăqôb (Jacob), from where the twelve tribes of Yâshârêl come out. Until that moment in history the people of **YAHUAH** or Yâshârêl had not been the slave of any nation.

When Yôsêph begins to have dreams from **YAHUAH,** his brothers, who were already jealous enough of him since Yaăqôb preferred him over the others because he was born from the love of his life Râchêl, for whom Yaăqôb had worked for 14 years, are even more jealous now with the dreams. **Berĕshîṯh 37**: *3 Now Yâshârêl (Yaăqôb) loved Yôsêph more than all his children, because he was the son of his old age: and he made him a coat of many colors.*

The zeal was so great that Yôsêph's brothers conceived a plan to kill him, but Reûbên did not allow it. **Berĕshîṯh 37**: *20-21 Come now therefore, and let us slay him, and cast him into some pit, and we will say, some evil beast has devoured him: and we shall* *see what will become of his dreams. ²¹ And Reûbên heard it, and he delivered him out of their hands; and said, Let us not kill him.*

Later his brother Yahûdâh (Judah) tried to prevent them from shedding his brother's innocent blood and finally they decided to sell him. **Berēshīṯh 37**: ²⁶⁻²⁷ *And Yahûdâh said unto his brethren, what profit is it if we slay our brother, and conceal his blood? ²⁷ Come, and let us sell him to the Yishmâêliy, and let not our hand be upon him; for he is our brother and our flesh. And his brethren were content.*

A very wise decision from Yahûdâh to avoid spilling the blood of his brother; however, they did not think at all about the future consequences of their actions. By this action of selling their brother into slavery, they were selling themselves and their offspring into slavery for almost 450 years.

It should be noted that the decision of Yahûdâh made him the person who would carry the chosen lineage of the Mâshîyach for the centuries to come and because the first three brothers to inherit the firstborn rights were discarded by his actions (Reûbên sleeps with his father's concubine, Shimôn and Lêwîy plotted and killed a whole town).

His brothers conceived the plan to enslave their brother the dreamer, however, **YAHUAH** used that plan to fulfill his purpose and the dreams he had shared with Yôsêph. But the decision of their brothers condemned them and all their descendants to slavery. It's a bit ironic!

This is my favorite story in the whole Bible and Yôsêph's character is my favorite, because I am amazed by Yôsêph's relationship with **YAHUAH**. Yôsêph simply trusted that whatever happened in his life was for a reason and that behind that reason his Creator **YAHUAH** would glorify himself.

The surprising thing is that there is no record at all of **YAHUAH** speaking directly to Yôsêph. **YAHUAH** didn't need to speak to Yôsêph, they both knew that the plan would be executed according to the will of **YAHUAH** and Yôsêph would accept that will, whatever it was. This is what we call a life of faith, or living by faith. It has always been by faith.

With this account we can clearly understand where the slaves came from; those whom **YAHUAH** sends to rescue from Mitsrayin (Mitsrayim) using Môsheh (Môsheh) as a liberating hand.

Sin and the Tôrâh (Law)

It is essential to understand what sin really means and what the Tôrâh represents in our lives. We hear many versions about the original sin and the conclusion that most people come to is that the sin was the eating of the forbidden fruit (it is not an apple).

Berēshīṯh 2: [16-17] *And YAHUAH ĔLÔHÎYM commanded Âdâm, saying, of every tree of the garden you may freely eat:* [17] *But of the tree of the knowledge of good and evil, you shall not eat of it: for in the day that you eat thereof you shall surely die.*

If we read carefully, Âdâm's sin was not actually the eating of the fruit that YAHUAH forbade him to eat. The eating of the fruit was the result of sin, not sin itself.

The real sin was disobedience. Man received his first commandment or Tôrâh and it was not to eat from the tree of the knowledge of good and evil.

Man disobeys the command of his Creator and as a result of breaking this Tôrâh his ordinance comes to eat the forbidden fruit.

Let me explain it in a more clear and contemporary way. You tell your son, *"Don't put your hands on the keys. They're my car keys and they're not for playing with. If you put your hands on him, I'll punish you"*. Something simple, simple and clear.

The moment your child puts his hands on the keys, you feel an anger, an anger and an impatience, because your child DISOBEYED your command. And you immediately proceed to reproach, punish and reiterate the command that you had given.

You want your child to obey your orders or commands, because you understand that, by obeying your command, he will be able to grow as a good man and in obedience. Disobedience is the part that makes us angry, it's not because of the keys, it's because he disobeyed our ordinances. This is the original sin and what led to the fall of all humanity: "disobedience."

I think we still do not understand or assimilate well what original sin or disobedience really is or means in our lives. Due to the original sin, we are all born with the mark of sin on our bodies, that is, from the moment we are conceived and come into this world, our faithful companion is the original sin or disobedience.

Why do you think that the first thing a child learns to say is NO? And our greatest job as parents is to teach our children obedience. For we were born with the sin of disobedience and we only want to do or live without law "in sin".

The child wants to do as he pleases all the time, he does not want to obey commands or ordinances; no matter how small any command we give him, he does not accept it because disobedience is the engine with which we are born.

And this original sin that is disobedience is present every day of our lives. When the child reaches adolescence, the situation is even worse, in fact, some call this stage as the stage of rebelliousness.

According to themselves, teenagers, they know more than everyone else, they are the only ones who are right and you can't call attention to them, because they get angry, they stamp their feet, they curse, they run away and they are completely rebellious, because they just want to do according to their whims. That is the manifestation in life of the original sin.

By the time we reach adulthood, we think that we are going to get rid of disobedience, but this is not the case because while we are in this earthly body, we will carry the original sin in us.

As adults we always want to be right and we always want others to do what we say, and in many cases we even create our own laws to live according to our opinion. We are disobedient and allergic to everything that is called law. This is human nature. This is the original sin at work in our entire existence.

However, we must understand and ask ourselves, disobedience to what? Disobedience to the Tôrâh that was given to us. But if we did not have that Tôrâh that was given to us, then there would be no sin or disobedience.

What exactly does this statement mean?

Obedience to the Tôrâh	=	Not sin
Disobedience to the Tôrâh	=	Sin

That is to say, that the Tôrâh was given to us (the Ten Commandments, their statutes and ordinances) to serve as a regulation to follow, to know and recognize the sin that is synonymous with disobedience. If we did not have the law, we would not know the meaning of sin.

Therefore, to obey the Tôrâh is to walk a sinless life and to disobey the law is to walk in a life of sin (disobedience). **Romans 3**: *²⁰ for by the works of the Tôrâh no human being will be justified in His sight (**YAHUAH**); for through the Tôrâh is the knowledge of sin.*

We need the Tôrâh to walk in obedience; the Tôrâh is our measure to know whether or not we are in sin. Keeping the Tôrâh keeps us out of sin, not keeping it keeps us in sin. **Romans 3**: *²⁴ being justified freely by his grace, through the redemption that is in the Mâshîyach **YAHUSHA**.*

The Tôrâh does not give us salvation, there is only salvation by **YAHUSHA,** who justifies us by his grace and redeems us from sin, can give us salvation and, as a result of that redemption or salvation in **YAHUSHA,** we keep His commandments and keep ourselves out of sin.

To those who say that the Tôrâh is no longer necessary or that it has gone out of fashion, I say, if it were so, how would you know what is sin and what is not? **2 Corinthians 5**: [20–21] *So, we are ambassadors on behalf of the Mâshîyach, as if ELOHIYM were pleading through us; we beseech you on behalf of the Mâshîyach: Be reconciled to* **YAHUAH**. [21] *He made him who knew no sin to be sin for us, that we might be made the righteousness of ELOHIYM in him.*

YAHUSHA knew NO sin because he always walked in obedience; however, he became a sinner for us in order to reconcile us to the Father **YAHUAH**. We need the Tôrâh to walk in obedience and without sin, and we need **YAHUSHA** to obtain salvation and eternal life.

The Ten Commandments

Let's look at the Ten Commandments according to the Bible since there are people who accept some of the commandments and others do not. We all understand that the commandments were the ordinances or rules given to Môsheh in **Šhemōṯh 20**. It is unbelievable to say that almost the entire human race, whether believer or not, accepts and believes in most of the commandments, which serve as a moral and civic guide in most countries of the world. I say in most part of the Ten Commandments because some people reject to believe in two of them. Let us review them below.

(יהוה) – CHAPTER II

● *³ You shall have no other gods before me*: The Hebrew term for you shalt not have is Hâyâh (הָיָה) which means to exist. In other words, YAHUAH says that there will be no one other than Him. **YAHUAH** is the only Creator and ELOHIYM of our lives. NO one and NOTHING else.

● *⁴ You shall not make unto you any graven image, or any likeness of anything that is in heaven above, or that is in the earth beneath, or that is in the water under the earth. ⁵ You shall not bow down yourself to them, nor serve them: for ¹ YAHUAH your ĚLÔHÎYM am a jealous ÊL (אֵל), visiting the iniquity of the fathers upon the children unto the third and fourth generation of them that hate me; ⁶ And showing mercy unto thousands of them that love me, and keep my commandments.*

● I do not understand what can be so difficult to understand, since all the terms and words used here are clear. No image of any kind should be honored, much less bowed down (prostrate, kneel, adore or venerate). Why? Because YAHUAH is jealous and does not share His creation with anyone, since He alone was the creator. So why break His commandment by following idols and images that they neither see nor feel...?

● *⁷ You shall not take the name of YAHUAH your ĚLÔHÎYM in vain; for YAHUAH (יהוה) will not hold him guiltless that takes his name in vain.*

● The word in Hebrew to define vain is Shâw (שְׁוְא) which means in the sense of desolation according to the Strong concordance...; *evil, ruin, or especially deceit; idolatry, uselessness, in vain: - false, lying, vanity.* In other words, taking His name in vain, it can

28

be: speaking badly with the intention of harming and destroying someone using His name. Using His name to deceive, lie, or in idolatry, pagan cults or rites.

● *⁸ Remember the Shabbâth day, to keep it holy. ⁹ Six days shall you labor, and do all your work: ¹⁰ But the seventh day is the Shabbâth of YAHUAH your ĔLÔHÎYM: in it you shall not do any work, you, nor your son, nor your daughter, your manservant, nor your maidservant, nor your cattle, nor your stranger that is within your gates:*

● It is the most violated and ignored commandment by almost all of humanity. Don't you know that the term or name Saturday, "Shabbath," means rest; however, we will talk more about this commandment in the section on keeping the Shabbath.

● ¹² Honor your father and your mother: that your days may be long upon the land which YAHUAH your ĔLÔHÎYM gives you: The whole world understands this commandment well and correctly.

● ¹³ *You shall not kill:* The whole world understands this commandment well and correctly.

● ¹⁴ *You shall not commit adultery:* I think this is the second most violated commandment in the history of mankind. However, there is an aspect about this commandment that some of us ignore, since we all think that committing adultery is only having sex outside of your marriage or with someone who is not your partner. And yes, this is the main concept, but the Hebrew term is Nâaph (נָאַף), which also translates as **"apostasy"**, means "to turn back", "to relapse" in the spiritual sense or "to turn one's back" to **YAHUAH**. So to commit adultery is also to

29

turn your back or turn away from **YAHUAH**.

- [15] *You shall not steal:* The whole world understands this commandment well and correctly.

- [16] *You shall not bear false witness against your neighbor:* The whole world understands this commandment well and correctly. But it is so violated that we could say that it is the third commandment most violated both implicitly and explicitly.

- [17] *You shall not covet your neighbor's house, you shall not covet your neighbor's wife, nor his manservant, nor his maidservant, nor his ox, nor his ass, nor any thing that is your neighbor's:* We all understand this commandment, but when we apply it, the reality of it escapes us and we forget that we should not covet, desire or lust for the things of others.

Of these Ten Commandments, *the Second and the Fourth* they are the most violated or ignored by humanity. People know that they should not have idols or images, much less worship them.

However, they ignore this commandment and come up with all kinds of cheap excuses to justify their sin. But in the end, I hope you can come to the biblical conclusion that with this practice you do not please at all **YAHUAH** and that you are transgressing the Second commandment given by **YAHUAH** for eternal obedience.

Even when the nations of the earth take the commandments as a guide to create their statutes and laws, something practically universal, they always distort and forget the fourth commandment to keep the Shabbath.

Keeping the Shabbath (*The Fourth Commandment*)

We will learn how the Roman Empire decided to change the Shabbath day (Saturday) for Sunday, an event that works for many as the main excuse to say that **YAHUSHA** abolished or fulfilled the Shabbath. So, those of short understanding prefer to fraudulently keep Sunday instead of Saturday.

The first thing we need to remember or consider about the Fourth Commandment to Keep the Shabbath is that it was a practice from the beginning of creation. **Berēshĭth 2**: [2]And on the seventh day ĔLÔHÎYM ended his work which he had made; and he rested on the seventh day from all his work which he had made. [3]And ĔLÔHÎYM blessed the seventh day, and sanctified it: because that in it he had rested from all his work which ĔLÔHÎYM created and made.

What we are saying is that the Shabbath was kept from **Berēshĭth 2** that is, the seventh day of the creation of the universe was the Shabbath. In conclusion, it was established about 2,500 years before the Tôrâh was given to Môsheh. In Šhemōṯh 20 we see the command to keep the Shabbath as the day of rest, thus reaffirming what the ancestors already practiced.

Jubilees 2: [19]*And He said to us, "Behold, I will set apart for myself one people from among all the peoples, and these **they will keep the Shabbath day** and I will sanctify them for Myself as My people,*

31

*and I will bless them; as I have **sanctified the Shabbath day** and I sanctify it for myself, so I will bless them, and they will be my people and I will be their ELOHIYM.*

We all understand the Shabbath commandment, however, there are those who say that it has already been fulfilled and that this commandment is from the Mosaic Law and that it should no longer be kept. It is obvious that all these assertions are false.

Yirmeyâhû 17: *21 Thus said **YAHUAH**; Take heed to yourselves, and bear **no burden on the Shabbâth day,** nor bring it in by the gates of Yerûshâlaim; 22 Neither carry forth a burden out of your houses **on the Shabbâth day**, neither do you any work, but hallow you **the Shabbâth day**, as I commanded your fathers.*

Yirmeyâhû 17: *27 But if you will not hearken unto me to **hallow the Shabbâth day**, and not to bear a burden, even entering in at the gates of Yerûshâlaim on **the Shabbâth day**; then will I kindle a fire in the gates thereof, and it shall devour the palaces of Yerûshâlaim, and it shall not be quenched.*

Yechezqêl 20: *12 Moreover also I gave them my Shabbâth, to be a sign between me and them that they might know that I am YAHUAH that sanctify them. 13 But the house of Yâshârêl rebelled against me in the wilderness: they walked not in my statutes, and they despised my judgments, which if a man do, he shall even live in them; and my Shabbâth they greatly polluted: then I said, I would pour out my fury upon them in the wilderness, to consume them.*

Yechezqêl 20: [16] *Because they despised my judgments, and walked not in my statutes, but polluted my Shabbâth: for their heart went after their idols.*

Yechezqêl 22: *Her kôhên have violated my tôrâh, and have profaned mine holy things: they have put no difference between the holy and profane, neither have they showed difference between the unclean and the clean, and have hid their eyes from my Shabbâth, and I am profaned among them.*

As we see in these few verses, the big problem (or the biggest problem) of Yâshârêl was forgetting Their Shabbath and that's why they always suffered the consequences. The controversy of forgetting the Shabbath Day is nothing new and comes from generation to generation. This is a practice that indicates the forgetting of the law of **YAHUAH** and apostasy (turning away from **YAHUAH**) in the lives of those who practice it.

The anger of **YAHUAH** is kindled on those who profane his Shabbath day. Some are not seeing it yet, but soon they will be able to see how they have been in an eternal blindness that only leads them to perdition for ignoring His laws and desecrating His Shabbath day.

Yechezqêl 20:16 it is the verse that best describes our generation and the world today, the One who has discarded His decrees and replaced them with the decrees of men. The world does not walk in the statutes of **YAHUAH** rather, walks in the statutes of its own lusts or in the statutes of pagan governments or rulers, which have nothing to do with **YAHUAH**.

The desecration of their Shabbath is so great that they changed it to Sunday. And finally, the heart of almost all mankind goes after pagan idols or Gods. How sad.

YAHUSHA and the Two Commandments

Many people say that **YAHUSHA** fulfilled the law and that of all the Ten commandments the only one he fulfilled was the fourth commandment to keep the Shabbath, so that, according to them, one should no longer keep the Shabbath.

However, if **YAHUSHA** has already fulfilled the commandments according to many, so is it lawful to kill? Is it legal to steal? Is it permissible to commit adultery? Is it lawful to have other Gods or to idolize? Is it lawful to covet? Is it lawful to bear false witness? Is it permissible to take the name of **YAHUAH** in vain? Is it lawful to dishonor our parents? According to the people, then YAHUSHA could only fulfill one commandment (to keep the Shabbath) and had no power to fulfill the others... What a great stupidity...

That's what those who say that the Shabbath should no longer be kept imply, that **YAHUAH** did send his Son to die for humanity in order to abolish ONLY ONE of the Ten Commandments that He gave to His people? (He never abolished them...) Or are you suggesting that the sacrifice of **YAHUSHA** was not enough to, according to you, abolish all the commandments? It is obvious that this alleged statement is completely false. No part of the New Testament states that **YAHUSHA** abolished the commandments.

YAHUSHA never came to abolish His Father's commandments (**YAHUAH)**, on the contrary, **YAHUSHA** came to show us that His commandments could be fulfilled. **John 14**: *15 If you love me, keep my commandments.*

We could fill several books with so many Biblical quotes that affirm that keeping the Shabbath is the Fourth Commandment and that it will always be valid, as well as the other nine commandments. If we say that he abolished the Shabbath, we are then saying that he abolished all the commandments. It's crazy to even think about it.

YAHUSHA, his disciples, the apostles and the early church kept the Shabbath. I will not talk about the other nine commandments because, apparently, the only commandment that everyone wants to allude to as abolished is the Shabbath, and believe me that those who claim this are more than blind.

In addition, it is interesting to note that the Shabbath is mentioned more than 50 times in the four Gospels; this is even more than what is mentioned in the first five books of the Old Testament.

The Pharisees were always trying to get **YAHUSHA** in trouble, for that reason and thanks to their short minds, they inquire about the commandments. However, **YAHUSHA** says in **Matthew 22**: *36 Teacher, what is the great commandment in the law? 37 **YAHUSHA** he said to him: You will love the **YAHUAH** your ELOHIYM with all your heart, and with all your soul, and with all your mind. 38This is the first and great commandment. 39And the second*

is similar: You shall love your neighbor as yourself.
⁴⁰On these two commandments the whole law and
the prophets depend.

Let's understand what it is that **YAHUSHA** is saying in these verses since, he never said that those are the only two new commandments nor that the other commandments are no longer valid. To say or think this is inconceivable and unacceptable to any thinking mind.

Loving a YAHUAH: If you love a **YAHUAH,** obviously you will not have other gods in your life, nor will you worship or have any image to venerate or worship it, much less to prostrate and pray to it since it is an action that **YAHUAH** hates. Similarly, you would also not take the name of **YAHUAH** in vain and surely would you keep His day of rest, that is, the Shabbath. This means that in this short sentence of **YAHUSHA** the first four commandments of **Šhemōṯh 20** are defined.

Love your neighbor as yourself: If you come to love your neighbor as yourself, then you will always honor your parents, you will never kill, you will not commit adultery, you will not steal, you will not raise false slanders and much less covet. This means that in this second sentence it refers to and includes the remaining six commandments. **Wayyīqrā (Leviticus)** 19:[18] *You shall not avenge, nor bear any grudge against the children of your people, **but you shall love your neighbor as yourself**: I am **YAHUAH**.* Not a new commandment, but firmly expressed since ancient times.

This is the thought of **YAHUSHA**, not the bad thinking that humanity has that the other commandments are already abolished. NO.

What **YAHUSHA** is telling you is that, if you really manage to fulfill these two commandments, you will be consequently fulfilling all the commandments of the law and the prophets. ***John 14***: *¹⁵ If you love me, keep my commandments.* And now I ask, what are the commandments of **YAHUSHA**?

It is obvious that the same commandments as those of the Father **YAHUAH**. Conversely, those who do not keep His commandments do not love Him. This is the reason why **YAHUSHA** says in **Matthew 15**: *This people honors me with their lips, but their heart is far from me.* Here he refers to those who are still blind and only honor our Creator with their lips **YAHUAH** and Salvador **YAHUSHA**.

Luke 4: *¹⁶He came to Nazareth (**YAHUSHA**), where he had been brought up; and on the Shabbath day he went into the synagogue, according to his custom, and rose up to read.*

There it clearly says on the Shabbath, that is, on the Shabbath or Day of rest he entered the synagogue according to his custom. What was the custom of **YAHUSHA**? To keep the Shabbath. I think the verse explains it clearly.

Mark 6: *He came out (**YAHUSHA**) from there he came to his own country, and his disciples were following him. ²And the Shabbath day has come (**Saturday**), and he began to teach in the synagogue; and many, when they heard him, wondered, and said, Whence has this man these things? And what is this* *wisdom that is given to him, and these miracles that are done by his hands?*

Luke 13: *¹⁰He was teaching (**YAHUSHA**) in a synagogue on the Shabbath day (**Saturday**).*

Luke 4: *³¹ He descended (**YAHUSHA**) to Capernaum, a city of Galilee; and he taught them on the Shabbath (**Saturday**).*

YAHUSHA, as the Savior of humanity or of what had been lost, he understood the purpose of the Shabbath and knew that it was an appropriate time to carry his message of healing, hope and redemption for humanity, and also to proclaim that message with his actions.

Luke 6: *¹It happened on a Shabbath day (**Saturday**), going on **YAHUSHA** through the fields, his disciples plucked ears of grain and ate, rubbing them with their hands.*

Some misinterpret many verses, including this one, to say that **YAHUSHA** broke or abolished the Shabbath; however, they are wrong. The disciples were hungry and plucked ears of grain and ate them, but this does not mean that the disciples were harvesting or performing the task of harvesting. If we read in **Debārīm 23**: *²⁵ When you come into the standing corn of your neighbor, then you may pluck the ears with your hand; but you shall not move a sickle unto your neighbor's standing corn.*

This is exactly what the disciples were doing. They never broke the Shabbath, as the Pharisees and the blind people of this time want to prove.

In fact, **YAHUSHA** introduced us to the original purpose of the Shabbath by returning to it as at the beginning: **YAHUAH** created the Shabbath as a time of blessing and true rest from daily chores, and not as a time of bitterness or heavy burden. **Matthew 11**: *30 for my yoke is easy, and my burden is light.* Saturday is a time to be enjoyed, not to spend it with bitterness and sorrow. It is a day to spend it as you most want and make you feel better, away from routine jobs. Moreover, the Shabbath was not a day of rest only for the nation of Yâshârêl, but for all mankind. 95% of the miracles and healings of **YAHUSHA** they were made on a Shabbath, not in order to break it, on the contrary, to show us the best way to keep the Shabbath.

I don't think it's necessary to include a bunch of Bible verses to prove the obvious; the disciples were walking with their teacher **YAHUSHA** therefore, they kept the Shabbath.

The apostles did the same, they also kept the Shabbath. **Acts 16:** *13 And a day of rest* (**Saturday**) *we went out outside the gate, by the river, where prayer used to be held; and sitting down, we spoke to the women who had gathered.* **Timothy, Paul and Silas**. It is clarified in case someone wants to say that they were not the apostles.

Acts 17: *2 And Paul, as his manner was, went in unto them, and three **Shabbath days** reasoned with them out of the scriptures...*

Acts 18: *4 And he was arguing* (**Paul**) *in the synagogue every Shabbath day* (**Saturday**), *and he persuaded Yahudiy and Greeks.*

Matthew 5: [17] *Do not think that I have come to destroy the law or the prophets; I have not come to destroy, but to fulfill*. [18]*For verily I say unto you, until heaven and earth pass away, not one drop nor one tittle shall pass from the law, until all things have been fulfilled*. [19]*Therefore whosoever shall break one of these very little commandments, and teach men so, shall be called very little in the kingdom of heaven: but whosoever shall do them, and teach them, the same shall be called great in the kingdom of heaven*. So be it!

These are proper and textual words of **YAHUSHA** that is, it is clearly said that he did not come to abolish, which is the same as abolishing, the Shabbath as a day of rest, but rather came to fulfill it. Moreover, he says that everything written in the law will be fulfilled to the letter and whoever does or keeps these commandments will be called great in the kingdom of heaven.

It is clear that the world does not listen to the word of **YAHUAH** because he says that **YAHUSHA** abolished them, but neither listen to the words of **YAHUSHA** since he commands us to fulfill what they say should no longer be kept. Who should we believe in? In men who are fallible or in **YAHUAH** what is eternal and infallible?

When did people start to forget about the Shabbath? As we have said before, the people of Yâshârêl have always been like all of us. In other words, when they were well, blessed and prospered, they turned away from **YAHUAH**, they forgot His statutes and profaned His day of rest (Shabbath). Consequently, they were handed over into the hands of their enemies or neighboring nations to be conquered and suffer the consequences of forgetting the laws, statutes and the Shabbath of **YAHUAH**.

Then, from the pit of despair they cried out and **YAHUAH** sent a deliverer, renewed His covenant with them, the people remembered the laws and statutes of **YAHUAH** and so they entered the cycle of blessings. This is basically the same story of all humanity; and it includes us, since we are not the exception.

Sometimes we criticize the people of Yâshârêl, but we do not notice that we act in the same way as they do. **YAHUSHA** came and set us free to live in harmony and communion with **YAHUAH**, but we are still in the same. Then, thanks to our disobedience and forgetfulness of the laws and statutes of **YAHUAH**, the biggest disappointment of all time came.

I will then tell you what happened briefly. The Emperor Constantine appeared with his dream of uniting the church with the state, and he did so. Two of the main goals and points of the new kingdom of the Roman Empire were to make sure that no one worshipped any other **ELOHIYM** but the **ELOHIYM** created by Constantine and his church.

As a consequence, those who kept the Shabbath and kept the feasts of **YAHUAH** they were considered heretics, persecuted, executed, burned, imprisoned and everything you already know. This was the origin of our century to forget the Fourth Commandment, so that Constantine and his empire decided that the day they should keep and consecrate was no longer Saturday, but Sunday. This was in honor of the pagan

ELOHIYM Mithras or the sun ELOHIYM.

CHAPTER III

---◈◆◈---

The Feasts of YAHUAH
(Biblical Feasts)

According to the Bible there are various holidays celebrated in honor and in commemoration of a special time or action by and for **YAHUAH**. Many people tend to believe that the Biblical Holidays were abolished or that they are no longer necessary to keep and celebrate today.

Everyone is free to believe as they like, however, we will be sharing the information about the *7 **Biblical Feasts*** and all holidays according to the bible for every year, a total of 70 days of holidays and the mandate of **YAHUAH** for us to celebrate them. By looking at the mandates of **YAHUAH,** everyone will be able to decide if they want to incorporate them into their life or not. For my part, I have the following reasoning that I want to share with every person who reads this short guide.

There are many pagan holidays in honor of pagan

deities and even humans. Everyone decides to celebrate all these feasts or holidays without any objection, inconvenience or restriction. However, I wonder, *which is more profitable, to celebrate the pagan holidays or to celebrate the* **YAHUAH's**?

Assuming that those who say that the **Feasts of YAHUAH** or **Biblical Festivals** were abolished or have already passed. *Why then do they only celebrate the pagan holidays? Is it more profitable to honor pagan god than to* **YAHUAH**? Everyone think for themselves and come to their own conclusion. I, for one, will celebrate and keep the **Feasts of YAHUAH**.

These are the main Bible holidays with their Bible verses so you can check and see for yourselves.

Some may wonder, why should we take the time to talk about the Holidays of **YAHUAH**?

Because in the seven Feasts of **YAHUAH** we can find the plan of redemption and salvation for all mankind. Understanding the Holidays will help us to have a better understanding of His master plan for us. In the same way, the biblical Feasts always have a historical aspect and an eschatological or futuristic aspect; moreover, they extend to all humanity until the last moment on this earth.

It is curious that the term used in Hebrew for the word Feast, in **Wayyiqrā 23**:[2] Speak *unto the children of Yâshârêl, and say unto them, concerning* ***the feasts of YAHUAH (יהוה)***, *which you shall proclaim to be holy convocations, even these are my feasts.*

Môêd (מוֹעֵד) is the term used and may mean, according to the Strong Bible Concordance H3259, *an appointment, specifically a festival, an assembly called for a definite purpose; place of meeting; also a sign as designated in advance: feast, allotted time.*

The holidays are a date with **YAHUAH** our Creator and their purpose is that we can come to know Him better and rejoice in His presence. It is a reminder for us to have an idea of the plan of Redemption that **YAHUAH** has prepared in advance and for an already assigned future time.

In verse 2 of **Wayyīqrā 23** he tells us something shocking, *The solemn feasts **from YAHUAH***. I do not know if we have fully understood, the holidays *whose are they?* These feasts belong to **YAHUAH**, not to us or to any man.

The Hebrew term "Môêd" is first used in **Berēshīth 1**: [14] *And **ĔLÔHÎYM** said, Let there be lights in the firmament of the heaven to divide the day from the night; and let them be for signs, and for <u>seasons</u>, and for days, and years:*

They have a historical character: because they present us with a time or activity in the past that originated them.

● **They have a prophetic character, that is, they point to the future:** because they point us to the Mâshîyach and the end of time.

● **They all talk about the Messiah (YAHUSHA):** because in them we find the advent of the Mâshîyach from when he was on earth and how he fulfilled the first feasts in his life.

● **They all have an agricultural context:** as the

people chosen by **YAHUAH** was a farming village, all the festivals revolve in a context of agriculture for a better understanding.

● **The seven feasts represent the seven days of creation:** Because in seven days everything was created, **YAHUAH** gives us seven holidays a year through the feasts, as a reminder of his creation and as a future fulfillment plan. There are still 63 more holidays that we will address shortly.

● **The seven feasts represent YAHUAH's plan of redemption:** Because they present to us the plan of redemption from **Berēshîṯh** to **Revelation**, reaching the fulfillment of the end times.

● **The holidays are in the Bible:** because according to **2 Timothy 3:**[16] *All Scripture is inspired by ELOHIYM...* and if all scripture is inspired by **YAHUAH**, so the holidays are in the Bible. Consequently, they are part of the inspiration of **YAHUAH**.

Let us remember what the Apostle Paul says in **Galatians 3**: [24]*So the law has been **our schoolmaster**, to bring us to the Mâshîyach, that we might be justified by faith*. The word used in Greek for schoolmaster is "paidagōgos (παιδαγωγός)", that is *"teacher or un tutor, instructor, school teacher."* What Paul is trying to tell us is that the law is our teacher that guides us until it leads us to the Mâshîyach and that the feasts are part of the law, therefore, they lead us and speak directly of our Redeeming Mâshîyach **YAHUSHA**.

Do we believe in the Law or the Torah? O do we believe in the doctrines or traditions of men? Do we believe that the Scriptures are inspired by **YAHUAH,** *or not*? These are questions that we should ask ourselves and reflect on the answer that we truly carry in our hearts. For if we truly believe that all Scripture is inspired by **YAHUAH** ELOHIYM, then we must believe in His Feasts, because according to the very words of **YAHUAH**, these feasts are His "**YAHUAH's**». Or do we not believe in the first five books of the Bible? Let's reflect on this question and be honest with ourselves.

The holidays are very important for **YAHUAH** and they talk directly about His beloved son, **YAHUSHA**, since **YAHUSHA**:

● Was born on Pentecost.

● Died on Passover or Pesach.

● Was buried on the feast of Unleavened Bread and was the first fruits of the resurrection.

● Sent His ruach (spirit) on the Pentecost or feast of weeks.

Yes **YAHUSHA** as the only child of **YAHUAH** came to fulfill his father's will and took the time to make these holidays a reality at the most important moments of his earthly life, we must understand then that this shows us that the goal of **YAHUSHA** is to fulfill each and every one of these holidays in your life. We are called to imitate the life of **YAHUSHA**, not the lives of men.

In each of the Holidays we will see the plan of redemption of **YAHUAH**. This will give us a better perspective on the importance of the holidays in our lives and for humanity.

Pesach (Passover) and Unleavened Bread (Matstsah)

Šhemōṯh 12 / Jubilees 48 - 49

Let us start by reading the events that took us to the night of the Passover with the people of Yâshârêl.

Jubilees 48:9-18

[9] The prince Mastema resisted before you and wanted to make you fall into Pharaoh's hands. He helped in the incantations that the Mitsrayim made comparing themselves to you. [10] We allowed them to commit evil, but we did not tolerate medicine being made by their hands. [11] YAHUAH struck them with evil sores, and they could not fight them, for we forbid them to perform a single miracle. [12] Prince Mastema was confounded at all the signs and wonders. When he started shouting at the Mitsrayim that you they pursued with all the might of Mitsrayim, with their chariots and horses and with all the multitude of the peoples of Mitsrayim. [13] I came between them and Yâshârêl. And we delivered him out of his hands and out of the hands of his people, and YAHUAH brought them out through the sea as through the dry land. [14] All the people who had gone out to pursue Yâshârêl

were thrown by **YAHUAH**, our **ELOHIYM**, into the sea, into the depths of the abyss, under the sons of Yâshârêl, just as the Mitsrayim had thrown their sons into the river. In a million he took revenge, and a thousand valiant paladins perished for every infant of the children of your people thrown into the river. [15] **On the fourteenth, fifteenth, sixteenth, seventeenth, and eighteenth** days Prince Mastema was bound and shut up, far from the sons of Yâshârêl, so that he could not slander them. [16] On **the nineteenth day** we released them to help the Mitsrayim and to persecute the people of Yâshârêl. [17] He hardened their hearts and strengthened them. But **YAHUAH**, our **ELOHIYM**, conceived it this way to strike the Mitzrayim and throw them into the sea. [18] And on the fourteenth we bound him, so that he would not slander the children of Yâshârêl on the day when they were going to ask the Mitsrayim for chattel and clothing, articles of silver, gold, and bronze, to plunder the Mitsrayim for the slavery they had violently imposed on them, for we did not take the children of Yâshârêl out of Mitsrayim naked.

Chapter 49

[1] Remember the command that **YAHUAH** has given you about Passover. Celebrate it at the right time, on the fourteenth of the first month, by sacrificing before sunset and eating at night, at sunset on the fifteenth, from the moment the sun goes down. [2] For on that night - the beginning of the festival and of rejoicing - you were sitting down to eat Passover in Mitsrayim, and the forces of the prince Mastema had been sent to kill all the firstborn in the land of Mitsrayim, from Pharaoh's son to the captive slave girl who is in the mill, as well as the animals. [3] This

*is the sign that **YAHUAH** gave them: In every house at the door of which they see the blood of an annual lamb, do not go in to kill, but pass by, so that all who are in the house may be saved, for the sign of the blood is at the door. ⁴ The forces of **YAHUAH** did as he commanded them, passing by all the sons of Yâshârêl, without reaching them the plague of destroying every life of animal, person or dog. ⁵ The plague was very great in Mitsrayim, and there was no house where he had not died, and there was weeping and crying. ⁶ Meanwhile all Yâshârêl was eating Pesach meat, drinking wine and praising, blessing and praising **YAHUAH**, the **ELOHIYM** of their fathers, ready to come out of the yoke of Mitsrayim and the evil slavery. ⁷ Remember this day all the days of your life, keep it every year all your life, once a year on its day, according to its law, without delaying a day from its date, or from month to month. ⁸ **For it is an eternal rule, engraved on the heavenly tablets for all the children of Yâshârêl**, let them celebrate it every year on its day, once a year, in all their generations without limit, for it is fixed forever.*

On the night of Passover, that same day in the evening, at dusk, the people sacrifice the lamb and put the sign of the blood on the lintel as protection of **YAHUAH**.

That same night, the village begins to celebrate Passover, however, the angel of death kills all the firstborn of the Mitsrayim.

Pharaoh sends for Môsheh and **Ahărôn** and lets the people go. Mastema is tied up (the adversary) for 5 days (14, 15, 16, 17,18), but on the 19th, Mastema is released and incites Pharaoh's heart to persecute **YAHUAH**'s people.

YAHUAH divides the sea, and the whole army of Mitsrayim is drowned, thus taking revenge on Mitsrayim for all the Hebrew children they had thrown into the river.

I recommend you to read the 12th chapter of **Šhemōṯh** and **Wayyīqrā 23** to get a better idea.

Wayyīqrā 23:4-8:

*These are the solemn feasts of **YAHUAH**, the holy convocations, which you shall summon in their times:* [4] These are the feasts of **YAHUAH**, even holy convocations, which you shall proclaim in their seasons. [5] In the fourteenth day of the first month (**Âbîyb**) at even is the **YAHUAH**'s Pesach. [6] And on the fifteenth day of the same month (**next day**) is the feast of Matstsâh (**second feast**) unto **YAHUAH**: seven days you must eat Matstsâh. [7] In the first day you shall have a holy convocation: you shall do no servile work therein (**no work**). [8] But you shall offer an offering made by fire unto **YAHUAH** seven days (**7 days not 8**): in the seventh day is a holy convocation: you shall do no servile work therein (**no work**).

The first feast leads to two feasts together. On the first night (14th of Âbîyb) the Passover is celebrated (unleavened bread, bitter herbs); but that first night is also the first night of the feast of Unleavened Bread. It is then a 7-day feast, not a 8-days feast.

They needed:

The blood of the Lamb: they sprinkled on the Lintel

of each one's door so that when the angel of death (Mastema) passed by and saw it, he would go on by and not hurt any of the people of Yâshârêl.

The bitter herbs: these were lettuce-like vegetables, symbolizing the sufferings or bitterness during the 430 years of slavery.

The unleavened bread: it meant that they were ready and in a hurry, that they had to rush out of Mitsrayim, which means that they did not have time to ferment.

The meat of the lamb: remember that they had to eat the meat of the lamb that very night (only the first night). Nothing could be left for the next day and they could not break any bones.

Shemōṯh 12: [8] *And they shall eat the flesh in that night, roast with fire, and with Unleavened Bread - Matstsâh; and with bitter herbs they shall eat it.*

Shemōṯh 12: [14] *And this day shall be unto you for a memorial; and you shall keep it a feast to* **YAHUAH** *throughout your generations; you shall keep it a feast by an* **ordinance forever***.*

Shemōṯh 12: [19] *Seven days shall there be no leaven found in your houses: for whosoever eats that which is leavened, even that soul shall be cut off from the congregation of Yâshârêl, whether he be a stranger, or born in the land.*

In verse 14 he tells us: *during your generations; by a perpetual statute.*

This is the definition of the term perpetual, *That lasts and stays forever.* I think we all understand then the term used in the Bible, in other words, it means *"**forever, eternally**»*. Therefore, I do not understand how it is that some say that these feasts were abolished, if in the Bible **YAHUAH** himself says that we should celebrate them forever.

In verse 19 he tells us that we should not have any leaven in our houses during those days. So let's look at the application of the Passover supper and unleavened bread today. As it says **YAHUAH,** it is a reminder of His wonders with His people.

Pesach also means the *"The Last Supper or Holy Supper"* that **YAHUSHA** celebrated with his disciples.

As **YAHUSHA** shed his blood for the forgiveness of our sins once and for all, and then he became the perfect sacrifice. We no longer need the blood of the lamb or the sacrifice of the lamb.

Pesach and Matstsah in the New Testament

Matthew 26: *[1] When **YAHUSHA** had finished all these words, he said to his disciples,[2] "You know that within two days Passover is being celebrated, and the Son of Man will be handed over to be sacrificed. [17] On the first day of the feast of unleavened bread, the disciples came to **YAHUSHA**, saying to him, "Where do you want us to prepare for you to eat the Passover?" [18] And he said, Go into the city to a certain man, and say to him, The Teacher says, My time is at hand; I will celebrate Passover at your house with my disciples. [19] And the disciples did as **YAHUSHA** commanded them, and prepared the Passover.*

Mark 14: *[12] On the first day of the feast of unleavened* bread, when they were sacrificing the Passover lamb, his disciples said to him, "Where do you want us to go and prepare for you to eat the Passover?" ¹³ And he sent two of his disciples and said to them, "Go into the city, and a man carrying a pitcher of water will meet you. Follow him. ¹⁴ And wherever he enters, say to the master of the house, 'The Master says, 'Where is the room where I am to eat Passover with my disciples?' ¹⁵ And he will show you a large upper room ready, prepared for us there. ¹⁶ His disciples went and entered the city, and found as he had told them, and they prepared the Passover.

Luke 2: ⁴¹ His parents went to Yerûshâlaim every year at the feast of Pesach. ⁴² and when he was twelve years old, they went up to Yerûshâlaim according to the custom of the feast.

Luke 22: ¹ Now the feast of unleavened bread, which is called Passover, was at hand. ² And the chief priests and the scribes sought how to put him to death; for they feared the people. ⁷ The day of unleavened bread came, in which the Passover lamb had to be sacrificed. ⁸ And **YAHUSHA** sent Peter and John, saying, Go, prepare the Passover for us, that we may eat it. ⁹ They said to him, "Where do you want us to prepare it?" ¹⁰ He said to them, "Behold, when you enter the city, a man carrying a pitcher of water will meet you. Follow him to the house where he will enter, ¹¹ and say to the householder of that house, 'The Teacher says to you, Where is the room where I am to eat Passover with my disciples?' ¹² Then he will show you a large upper room ready; prepare there. ¹³ So they went and found as he had told them, and they prepared the Passover. ¹⁴ And when the hour was come, he sat down to meat, and the apostles with him. [15] And he said to them, How I have longed to eat this Pesach with you before I suffer! [16] For I tell you, I will eat it no more, until it is fulfilled in the kingdom of **ELOHIYM**. [17] And when he had taken the cup, he gave thanks, and said, Take this, and divide it among yourselves. [18] for I tell you, I will drink no more of the fruit of the vine, until the kingdom of **ELOHIYM** comes. [19] And he took bread, and gave thanks, and brake it, and gave to them, saying, This is my body, which is given for you: do this in remembrance of me. [20] In the same way, after he had supped, he took the cup, saying, "This cup is the new covenant in my blood, which is being poured out for you."

John 2: [13] The Passover of the Yahudiy was at hand; and **YAHUSHA** went up to Yerûshâlaim. [23] While he was in Yerûshâlaim at the feast of Passover, many believed in his name, seeing the signs that he was doing.

John 6: 4 And the Passover, the feast of the Yahudiy, was at hand.

John 13:1-30 [1] Before the feast of Passover, **YAHUSHA**, knowing that his hour had come for him to pass from this world to the Father, as he had loved his own who were in the world, loved them to the end.

Acts 20: [6] And we, when the days of unleavened bread were past, sailed from Philippi, and in five days we joined them at Troas, where we stayed seven days. [7] On the first day of the week, when the disciples were gathered together to break bread, Paul was teaching them, having to go out the next *day. And he continued his discourse until midnight.*

Acts 12: *³ And when he saw that this had pleased the Yahudiy, he proceeded to take Peter also. Those were the days of unleavened bread.*

Acts 18: *²⁰ and they besought him that he would tarry with them a while longer; but he would not consent, ²¹ but took leave of them, saying, At all events I must keep the coming feast in Yerûshâlaim; but I will return to you again, if **ELOHIYM** wills. And he sailed from Ephesus.*

1 Corinthians 5: *⁶ Your boasting is not good. Don't you know that a little yeast leavens the whole dough? ⁷ Cleanse yourselves therefore of the old leaven, that you may be a new dough, unleavened as you are; for our Passover, which is the Messiah, has already been sacrificed for us. ⁸ **So let's celebrate the feast**, not with the old leaven, nor with the leaven of malice and wickedness, but with unleavened bread, of sincerity and truth.*

Matthew 26: *²⁶And while they were eating, he took **YAHUSHA** the bread, and blessed, and broke it, and gave to his disciples, and said, Take, eat; this is my body. ²⁷And he took the cup, and when he had given thanks, he gave to them, saying, Drink of it, all of you; ²⁸ for this is my blood of the new covenant, which is shed for many for the remission of sins. ²⁹And I tell you that from now on I will no longer drink of this fruit of the vine, until that day when I drink it new with you in my Father's kingdom (**YAHUAH**).*

Let us recapitulate the final events of the earthly life of the Messiah.

Âbıyb 14: The Messiah is captured, just after celebrating Passover with his disciples. He is tried and found guilty by Caiaphas the high priest, the scribes and the elders. Now the chief priests, and elders, and all the council, sought false witness against **YAHUSHA**, to put him to death;

Âbıyb 15: YAHUSHA is whipped and at 9am (at the third hour of the day). When the morning was come, all the chief priests and elders of the people took counsel against **YAHUSHA** to put him to death: and delivered him to Pontius Pilate the governor. And they stripped him, and put on him a scarlet robe, crown of thorns on his head, and a reed in his right hand: And they spit upon him, and took the reed, and smote him on the head. And after that they had mocked him, they took the robe off from him, and put his own raiment on him, and led him away to impale him. Cyrene, Simon helped him with the stake and they impaled him. Now from the sixth hour (12:00 midday) there was darkness over all the land unto the ninth hour (3pm). By the ninth hour (3pm) they gave him vinegar to drink mingled with gall. Then **YAHUSHA** died by the end of that day. Before 6pm put in the tomb and anointed before 6am.

Âbıyb 16: the first day in the grave

Âbıyb 17: second day in the grave

Âbıyb 18: third day in the grave. The Messiah rises in the early morning, just before sunrise 6am. The Messiah is resurrected on the Shabbath or Saturday (never on Sunday).

Âbıyb 19: the tomb is empty, the Messiah rises on the third day, therefore on Saturday and not on the fourth day which would be Sunday. Peter is informed of the resurrection while the disciples are in hiding.

This means that:

The sacrifice or meat of the lamb is no longer necessary because **YAHUSHA** it was the perfect sacrifice.

The blood of the lamb is no longer needed because **YAHUSHA** poured it out once and for all and for the forgiveness of our sins. Now instead of the blood we use the wine, as **YAHUSHA** did so, thus representing the blood shed for each of us. Remember that we use unfermented wine because during those holidays nothing that contains yeast should remain or be used in our houses; as everyone will know, fermented wine contains yeast.

However, there is an even more dangerous yeast that is the internal yeast. This means that any bitterness, enmity, grudge, quarrel or strife should be removed from our lives during these celebrations.

The unleavened bread represents to us the body of **YAHUSHA** that was delivered for us.

Regarding bitter herbs, they will always represent the bitterness, pains, vicissitudes and hard work that we have gone through in our lives. At that moment we are handing them over to **YAHUSHA**.

So, at this time we celebrate the Passover and Unleavened Bread:

With bitter herbs (vegetables), unleavened breads and unfermented wine.

Remember that this is a celebration, a reminder or feast of **YAHUAH.** This means that, after having performed the rituals of *eating the bread* (body of **YAHUSHA** or the sign that we are ready for His coming, just as the people of Yâshârêl were, that is, ready to come out of slavery in Mitsrayim) and from *eating the bitter herbs* (in remembrance of the sufferings that the people of Yâshârêl went through in the 430 years of slavery in Mitsrayim and of the sufferings that they went through **YAHUSHA.**

In addition to the sufferings we have gone through in our lives waiting to be released from them) and *of drinking the wine* (in memory of how the blood of the lamb saved all the firstborn of Yâshârêl and not a single one died, and how the blood of **YAHUSHA** freed us from the slavery of sin, thus giving us eternal life in himself), we are incorporating into our lives the true meaning of this feast and it is, then, from that moment that we can follow with a gala dinner or any type of celebration or event that you think pertinent.

Let us not forget that that night the people of Yâshârêl were set free by the sign of the blood of the lamb on the lintel of the gate, but all the firstborn Mitsriy (Egiptian) died. In the same way as the blood of **YAHUSHA** was poured out for the forgiveness of our sins, we can celebrate our feast with a gala dinner (that's how I do it) and share with everyone present Biblical stories and anecdotes, always remembering the greatness of our Creator **YAHUAH** and of our Savior **YAHUSHA**. This is a feast of joy that is celebrated for 7 days. In 2024 the Feast of Passover and Unleavened Bread was from April 2 to April 9 (on the calendar that everyone uses, that is, the Gregorian one).

Some may be wondering how they should celebrate these Holidays of **YAHUAH or Biblical Feasts**. We should celebrate them with joy, as we are remembering the greatness of **YAHUAH** our **ELOHIYM**. In my case, I prepared a banquet every day of the feast, during the 7 nights. I organized the main banquet on the first and last night of the feast for the delight and enjoyment of the whole family and gathered guests.

Plan of Redemption: on the first day the salvation of all the firstborn of Yâshârêl is celebrated; it is a reflection of the future advent that was the Passover lamb **YAHUSHA** and that was delivered by us (***he died at this feast).*** In the same way, it leads us to long to celebrate this feast with our Savior **YAHUSHA once again**.

● **Historical application:** The liberation of Yâshârêl from slavery in Mitsrayim (Egipto).

● **Future application:** Death of **YAHUSHA** on the cross.

● **Spiritual application:** Faith and repentance in the blood of **YAHUSHA**.

The Plan of Redemption in the Unleavened Bread: It begins on the very night of the Passover feast, since, the next morning, the people of Yâshârêl were freed from the yoke of slavery. This feast takes us back to **YAHUSHA** and he reminds us of the suffering when he took the whole weight of humanity on his men to give his life for us (***he was resurrected during this feast***). We remember the time of slavery and vicissitudes with the expectation that soon our Creator **YAHUAH** and our Savior **YAHUSHA** will free us from every eternal yoke by dwelling in the New Yerûshâlaim.

● **Historical application:** The departure of the people of Yâshârêl from Mitsrayim or liberation from slavery, and the crossing of the Red Sea.

● **Future application:** Burial and resurrection of **YAHUSHA** (a first fruit from the dead).

● **Spiritual application:** Purification and separation from the bad things in our life, and beginning of a new life in **YAHUSHA**, the Mâshîyach.

The Feast of Shâbûa (Pentecost)

Wayyîqrā 23:9-16, Šhemōṯh 34:22, Šhemōṯh 23:16, Bemiḏbar 28:26, Jubilees 6:15-21.

This is one of the biggest holidays in the Bible and is known under different names: *Feast of Weeks, Feast of Harvests and Feast of First Fruits.*

Let us first see the origin of this feast when Nôach and his sons came out of the ark in the book of **Jubilees 16:15-21 & 24:**

15. And He gave to Nôach and his sons a sign that there should not again be a flood on the earth. 16. He set His bow in the cloud for a sign of the eternal covenant that there should not again be a flood on the earth to destroy it all the days of the earth. 17. For this reason it is ordained and written on the *heavenly tablets, **that they should celebrate the feast of weeks** in this month once a year, **to renew the covenant every year**. ^{18.} **And this whole festival was celebrated in heaven from the day of creation till the days of Nôach**, twenty six jubilees and five weeks of years: and Nôach and his sons observed it for seven jubilees and one week of years, till the day of Nôach's death, and from the day of Nôach's death his sons did away with (it) until the days of Abrâhâm, and they eat blood. ^{19.} But Abrâhâm observed it, and Yitschâq and Yaăqôb and his children observed it up to your days, and in your days the children of Yâshârêl forgot it until you celebrated it anew on this mountain. ^{20.} And do you command the children of Yâshârêl to observe this festival in all their generations for a commandment unto them: one day in the year in this month they shall celebrate the festival. ^{21.} For it is **the feast of weeks and the feast of first fruits**: this feast is twofold and of a double nature: according to what is written and engraved concerning it, celebrate it. **And Nôach ordained them for himself as feasts for the generations for ever**, so that they have become thereby a memorial unto him.*

There are many things that we don't know or that we are not told about the feast of weeks or Pentecost. As you can see, it is dated back the days of creation, meaning Âdâm was the first to celebrated and then Nôach and it was lost with the children of **YAHUAH** whenever they went astray. The purpose of this feast has always been to renew our vows or covenant with **YAHUAH**.

Âdâm kept it, Nôach kept it by renewing his covenant, Abrâhâm kept it by renewing his covenant, Yitschâq is born and kept it by renewing his covenant, Yaăqôb kept it by renewing his covenant, Môsheh kept it by renewing his covenant and teaching the people to celebrate it, **YAHUSHA** is born on this feast and is the perfect sacrifice for the new covenant renewal.

The Hebrew word Shâbûa means weeks, this is why it is the *Feast of the Weeks*. It is an anticipation of excitement and waiting since from the last Saturday of the feast of Unleavened Bread the "omer" count begins. This is how we can determine the day for this feast.

Wayyīqrā 23: *¹⁵ And you shall count unto you from the morrow after the Shabbâth, from the day that you brought the sheaf of the wave offering; seven Shabbâth shall be complete: ¹⁶ Even unto the morrow after the seventh Shabbâth shall you number fifty days; and you shall offer a new meat offering unto* **YAHUAH (יהוה)**.

We must count seven Shabbath starting from the last Shabbath of the feast of Unleavened Bread, that is, 7 weeks (7 x 7=49) and the next day (day 50) is the great feast. This is why it is also called Pentecost; the word comes from the Greek πεντηκοστή, (pentecost) meaning "fiftieth or 50th". This is the reason why this feast always falls on a Sunday, because we count the 7 Saturdays and the next day is the feast.

Wayyīqrā 23: *²¹And you shall call a holy convocation on this very day; you shall do no servile work* **(not working)***; perpetual statute* **(it is forever)** *wherever you live throughout your generations.*

This is the farmers' holiday. The people of Yâshârêl began their harvest right after the Feast of

Unleavened Bread, and then they had seven weeks to complete the harvest time and have it ready to be able to bring the first fruits of their harvests as an offering to **YAHUAH**.

Since the farmers had to move from their dwellings to the temple in Yerûshâlaim, it was a pilgrimage holiday for the people of Yâshârêl.

Wayyīqrā 23: [22] *When you reap the harvest of your land, you shall not reap to the uttermost corner of it, nor glean your harvest; you shall leave it for the poor and for the stranger. I* **YAHUAH** *your* **ELOHIYM**.

That is why this feast also serves to donate and help the poor and the homeless. It is a festival where the tributes and offerings to **YAHUAH** they come from our work, that's why part of the product of our work we donate to the poor and the foreigners as a sign or reminder of the blessings that **YAHUAH** gives us.

Acts 2: [2] *And suddenly there came a sound from heaven as of a rushing mighty ruach, and it filled all the house where they were sitting.* [3] *And there appeared unto them cloven tongues like as of fire, and it sat upon each of them.* [4] *And they were all filled with the Rûach Qôdesh, and began to speak with other tongues, as the rûach gave them utterance.*

The disciples were celebrating the feast, all the people of Yâshârêl were scattered among other peoples or nations who were coming or making pilgrimages to celebrate this solemn feast. It is at that moment that the disciples are in the room under the ordinance of **YAHUSHA** who had told them to wait for the Rûach (spirit) of **ELOHIYM** that would be given to them.

It was then that they received the Rûach of **ELOHIYM** on the day of Pentecost (new covenant), and as there were Yâshârêl coming from all the nations where they had scattered, the disciples began to speak in different tongues (languages) and each one heard them speak in their native language.

For us today this is the feast of Pentecost. As most of us are not farmers and we no longer grow fruits but have office jobs, our best offering to **YAHUAH ELOHIYM** it is our heart, our life, our time and our devotion in celebrating this feast that recalls the things He does every day in our lives and what He has done during the year. It is a great celebration with all kinds of fruits of the harvest, with wine, music, dance and joy. It is usually a feast that extends throughout the day, because it is a feast of salvation where people can give their lives to **YAHUSHA**. In the Biblical calendar for 2024 this feast falls on May 26. It is the day to renew your covenant with **YAHUAH**.

Plan of Redemption: We celebrate the blessings, harvests and fruits that **YAHUAH** has given us. On the eve of this feast, **YAHUSHA** ascends to heaven and begins his reign as our high priest. He demonstrated his success in the mission the Father gave him and set the pattern for his return to earth. Finally, during this feast, the advent of the Rûach of **ELOHIYM** came true.

● **Historical application:** Blessings of the harvests and celebrating of the new covenant in the Mount Sîynay.

● **Future application:** Manifestation or coming of

the Ruach of **ELOHIYM** in human hearts.

● **Spiritual application:** Growth and knowledge in the new Faith. The renewal of our covenant with **YAHUSHA**.

Feast of the Trumpets
Wayyīqrā 23:23-25, Bemīdbar. 29:1-6

This is the fourth feast of the year that **YAHUAH** tells us to celebrate in remembrance and honor of the great things that **YAHUAH** has done and is doing in our lives. The Feast of Trumpets is an alarm of war, a warning of peace.

Wayyīqrā 23: [24] Speak unto the children of Yâshârêl, saying, in the seventh month, in the first day of the month, you shall have a Shabbâth, a memorial of **blowing of trumpets,** a holy convocation. [25] You shall do no servile work therein (**No work**): but you shall offer an offering made by fire unto **YAHUAH** (**יהוה**).

The sound of the trumpets is used to transmit important messages, that is, a call to a meeting, the mobilization of the people, the sound of celebrations or joy.

Now, if we go back to the New Testament, we see that the sound of trumpets announces the coming of **YAHUSHA** or his return to find his people.

1 Thessalonians 4: [16]*Because **YAHUSHA** himself with a commanding voice, with the voice of an archangel, and **with YAHUAH's trumpet**, will* *descend from heaven; and the dead in the* **Mâshîyach** *they will be resurrected first.* [17]

This is a day of great joy where we remember the warnings of the apocalypse and the second coming of our Savior **YAHUSHA**.

Matthew 24: [30]*Then the sign of the Son of Man will appear (***YAHUSHA***) in heaven; and then all the tribes of the earth will mourn, and they will see the Son of Man (***YAHUSHA***) coming on the clouds of heaven, with power and great glory.* [31]*And he will send his angels* **with a great trumpet voice** *and they (angels) will gather together his chosen ones from the four winds, from one end of the sky to the other.*

1 Corinthians 15: [52]*in a moment, in the blink of an eye,* **to the final trumpet**; *because* **the trumpet will be blown**, *and the dead will be raised incorruptible, and we will be transformed.*

The Feast of Trumpets is of the utmost importance today and in the future. When we celebrate it, we must remember the future events evoked by the feast of trumpets since we are announcing the coming of **YAHUSHA**.

At the sound of the seventh trumpet, the Mâshîyach returns and the trumpet awakens those who are asleep and are resurrected in **YAHUSHA**.

Revelation 11: [15]*And the seventh angel sounded; and there were great voices in heaven, saying, The kingdoms of this world are become the kingdoms of our* **YAHUAH**, *and of his Mâshîyach; and he shall reign for ever and ever.*

The trumpets call us to wake up, give us a shout for war or announce the battle and warn us that there is danger. They also indicate repentance and the second coming.

Âmôs 3: *6 Shall a trumpet be blown in the city, and the people not be afraid? Shall there be evil in a city, and **YAHUAH** has not done it?*

Isaiah 27: *13 And it shall come to pass in that day, that the great trumpet shall be blown, and they shall come which were ready to perish in the land of Ashshûr, and the outcasts in the land of Mitsrayim, and shall worship **YAHUAH** in the holy mount at Yerûshâlaim.*

The sound of the trumpets will also serve to summon or gather all the followers of **YAHUAH** from the four ends of the earth in order that they may come to unite in worshipping to the Creator of the universe.

This is a feast in which we are called to bring a sweet-smelling offering to **YAHUAH**, so our heart and willingness to celebrate His feast and make it a reality in our lives is one of the best offerings we can give on this day of joy. In addition to blowing the trumpets or the sound of the trumpets on this day, we can share the scriptures and information about the coming of **YAHUSHA** during a family dinner or with our guests. This holiday falls on September 16, 2024.

Plan of Redemption: This feast announces to us that the kingdom of **YAHUAH** is near and reminds us of the second coming of **YAHUSHA** for his people. He also warns us against the danger of having him for delay or forgetting his return, presents us with the end of the last harvest at the end of time when his elect will be gathered from all corners of the earth, and finally reminds us of the judgments that are to come and the trumpets of revelation.

● **Historical application:** Sound and reminder to be prepared for war.

● **Future application:** Announcing the second coming of **YAHUSHA** and the resurrection of the dead to come.

● **Spiritual application:** To hear the call to repentance in our lives and to remember that the end is near.

Feast or Day of Atonement (Yôm Kippûr)

Wayyiqrā 23:27

Wayyiqrā 23: *²⁷ Also on the tenth day of this seventh month there shall be a **Yôm Kippûr**: it shall be a holy convocation unto you; and **you shall afflict your souls**, and offer an offering made by fire unto **YAHUAH (יהוה)**. ²⁸And you shall do no work in that same day: for it is a day of atonement, to make an atonement for you before **YAHUAH (יהוה)** your **ĔLÔHÎYM (אֱלֹהִים)**. ³² It shall be unto you a Shabbâth of rest, and you shall afflict your souls: in the ninth day of the month at even, **from even unto even**, shall you celebrate your Shabbâth.*

This is a feast of **Fasting and reconciliation** with **YAHUAH** and **YAHUSHA**. **It is a day of fasting,** *prayer and reading the word of YAHUAH*. This feast is observed from evening to evening, in other words, it begins at dusk on the first day and ends at dusk on the next day. On this day, there is no food because it is a day of affliction of our souls and of getting closer to our Creator **YAHUAH** and Salvador **YAHUSHA**. This feast is the ultimate reminder that **YAHUSHA** paid the offering or sacrifice of our sins once and for all.

It is a day of *covenant and reconciliation; renewing our vows with YAHUAH*, we are renewing our contract of acceptance and following His word in our lives. This feast of Yôm Kippûr or day of affliction of our souls falls on September 25, 2024.

Plan of Redemption: After keeping us alert and giving us the feast trumpets and reminding us of His coming, he prepares us for the day of affliction of our souls. It is the day of renewal of our covenant with **YAHUAH**, of fasting, prayer and reading of the word. Here we repent of our sins and seek His forgiveness and reconciliation, and return to obedience of His laws.

● **Historical application:** The High priest enters the most holy place for the forgiveness of the people's sin.

● **Future application:** The Coming of our High Priest and Savior **YAHUSHA** for his people.

● **Spiritual application:** Giving of our lives in faith to receive eternal life in **YAHUSHA** our Savior.

Feast of Tabernacles or Sukkot

Wayyīqrā 23:34-36 / Jubilees 16:21-31

This is one of the three largest feasts in the Bible; it lasts 7 days or a week and two feasts are celebrated instead of one. These are the last two Biblical feasts of the year.

The origin of this feast was Abrâhâm, the first one on earth to celebrate this feast according to the book of **Jubilees 16**: *[21] And he built there an altar to **YAHUAH** who had delivered him, and who was making him rejoice in the land of his sojourning, and he celebrated a festival of joy in this month seven days, near the altar which he had built at the Well of the Oath. [22] And he **built booths** for himself and for his servants on this festival, **and he was the first to celebrate the feast of tabernacles on the earth**. [25] And he celebrated this feast during seven days, rejoicing with all his heart and with all his soul, **he and all those who were in his house, and there was no stranger with him, nor any that was uncircumcised**. [29] For this reason **it is ordained on the heavenly tablets** concerning Yâshârêl, that they shall celebrate **the feast of tabernacles seven days with joy**, in the seventh month, acceptable before **YAHUAH**, a statute forever throughout their generations every year. [31] And Abrâhâm took branches of palm trees, and the fruit of goodly trees, and every day going round the altar with the branches seven times a day in the morning, he praised and gave thanks to his **ELOHIYM** for all things in joy.*

From these verses in the book of Jubilees we can see

how Abrâhâm celebrated the Feast of Tabernacles and how it was established in the heavenly tablets as an ordinance forever.

Wayyīqrā 23: ³⁴ *Speak unto the children of Yâshârêl, saying, the fifteenth day of this seventh month shall be the **feast of Sûkkâh** for seven days unto* **YAHUAH (יהוה)**. ³⁵ *On the first day shall be a holy convocation:* **you shall do no servile work therein**. ³⁶ *Seven days you shall offer an offering made by fire unto* **YAHUAH (יהוה)**: **on the eighth day shall be a holy convocation unto you**; *and you shall offer an offering made by fire unto* **YAHUAH (יהוה)**: *it is a solemn assembly;* **and you shall do no servile work therein**.

The Feast of Tabernacles is one of the most exciting holidays in the Bible. We get to experience what it's like to dwell or live in tabernacles, "tents or booths," for seven days.

Wayyīqrā 23: ⁴⁰ *And you shall take you on the first day the boughs of goodly trees, branches of palm trees, and the boughs of thick trees, and willows of the brook; and you shall rejoice before* **YAHUAH** *your* **ĔLÔHÎYM** *seven days.* ⁴¹ *And you shall keep it a feast unto* **YAHUAH** *seven days in the year.* **It shall be a statute forever in your generations**: *you shall celebrate it in the seventh month.* ⁴² *You shall dwell in booths seven days; all that are Yâshârêl born shall dwell in booths:* ⁴³ *That your generations may know that I made the children of Yâshârêl to dwell in booths, when I brought them out of the land of Mitsrayim: I am* **YAHUAH** *your* **ĔLÔHÎYM**.

The idea of this holiday is to build or erect tents and

dwell in them for seven days; we can make them in our yard, go to a mountain, and go to the countryside or wherever we feel more comfortable. The purpose is that we use the tents, huts or camps as a reminder to our children and all the coming generations of the wonders **YAHUAH** has done for all of us.

The Feast of Tabernacles also has a future ramification, **Zekaryâhû 14**: *16 And it shall come to pass, that every one that is left of all the nations which came against Yerûshâlaim shall even go up from year to year to worship the King, **YAHUAH Tsâbâ**, and to keep **the feast of Sûkkâh.** 17 And it shall be, that whoso will not come up of all the families of the earth unto Yerûshâlaim to worship the King, **YAHUAH Tsâbâ**, even upon them shall be no rain. 18 And if the family of Mitsrayim go not up, and come not, that have no rain; there shall be the plague, wherewith **YAHUAH** will smite the heathen that come not up to keep **the feast of Sûkkâh**. 19 This shall be the punishment of Mitsrayim, and the punishment of all nations that come not up to keep **the feast of Sûkkâh**.*

Hôshêa 12:*9 And I that am **YAHUAH** your **ĔLÔHÎYM** from the land of Mitsrayim will yet make you to dwell in tabernacles, as in the days of the solemn feast.*

Revelation 21: *3And I heard a great voice from heaven saying, Behold the **tabernacle of YAHUAH** with men, and he will dwell with them; and they will be his people, and **YAHUAH** himself will be with them as their **ELOHIYM**.*

These are prophetic verses telling us that **YAHUAH** will make us dwell in tabernacles as in the feasts and celebrate them. This means that those who do not celebrate them will suffer devastating consequences. And even more important is that when **YAHUSHA** start his millennial reign, all the nations of the earth will go up to Yerûshâlaim to celebrate the Feast of Tabernacles.

And at the end of all time in **Revelation 21**, John tells us about the new heaven and the new earth, the new Yerûshâlaim; he tells us that **YAHUAH** himself will dwell with us in His tabernacle, thus making reference to the feast of tabernacles. *How is it possible that many people say that this feast has already passed?* Maybe we're not reading the same Bible then. The Feast of Tabernacles is the last feast of the year and is the most important; it is a feast of joy and rejoice with our Creator **YAHUAH** and our Savior **YAHUSHA**.

In conclusion, at this feast we are going to have fun with **YAHUAH** using tree branches, palm trees; let's take that moment to build or set up the tents with our children or relatives. We can also build the tent or camp in wood and make a roof of palm branches. It is a unique experience in which we can cook outdoors and in fire pits or stones as our ancestors did. This holiday falls on October 1-8, 2024.

Feast of the Eighth Day

Wayyīqrā 23:39 / Jubilees 32:27-29

As stated before, there were seven days in the feast of tabernacles; however, Yaăqôb added an extra days according to the book of Jubilees and as per the instructions of **YAHUAH**.

Jubilees 32:27-29: *27 And he celebrated there yet another day, and he sacrificed thereon according to all that he sacrificed on the former days, and called its name "Addition" for this day was added and the former days he called 'The Feast. 28 And thus it was manifested that it should be, and it is written on **the heavenly tablets**: wherefore it was revealed to him that he should celebrate it, and add it to the seven days of the feast.*

This addition is what we called the feast of the eight day in **Wayyiqrā 23.** Therefore, the feast of tabernacles is extended until the 8th day.

Wayyiqrā 23: *39 Also in the fifteenth day of the seventh month, when you have gathered in the fruit of the land, you shall keep **a feast** unto **YAHUAH seven days**: on the first day shall be a Shabbâth, and **on the eighth day shall be a Shabbâth**.*

Our Savior and his disciples also celebrated these feasts; we can see it in the following Biblical quote in

John 7: *2 &37* Now the Yahudiy's **feast of tabernacles** was at hand. ***On the last and great day of the feast, YAHUSHA** he stood up and lifted up his voice, saying, "If anyone is thirsty, let him come to me and drink." 38Whoever believes in me, as the Scripture says, rivers of living water will flow from within him. 39This he said of the Ruach, which those who believed in him were to receive; for the Ruach of **ELOHIYM** had not yet come, because **YAHUSHA** he had not yet been glorified.*

This last and great day of the feast refers to the last day of the Feast of Tabernacles; it is the great closing and culmination day of the Biblical feasts of that year. On this day we return from the feast of tabernacles to our normal abode.

Revelation 21:1-3: *And I saw a **new heaven and a new earth**: for the first heaven and the first earth were passed away; and there was no more sea. ²And I John saw the **holy city, New Yerûshâlaim**, coming down from **ELOHIYM** out of heaven, prepared as a bride adorned for her husband. ³And I heard a great voice out of heaven saying, Behold, **the tabernacle of ELOHIYM** is with men, and **he (YAHUSHA)** will dwell with them, and they shall be his people, and **ELOHIYM** himself shall be with them, and be their **ELOHIYM**.*

Don't you know what **YAHUSHA** is our Tabernacle? Don't you see how important the feast of Tabernacles is in our lives?

For this reason, the eighth day is considered the big day, because it is the closing or culmination of this important and exciting festival of **YAHUAH** in our lives. This day falls on October 8, 2024.

Plan of Redemption: It shows us the coming down **of YAHUSHA** as our tabernacle in the millennial kingdom of our Savior. This is the final feast or big feast where we will be with our Creator **YAHUAH** and our Savior **YAHUSHA.** At this moment there will be no more crying, no more pains, no more fears, because it will be our eternal redemption and dwelling in **YAHUSHA**.

● **Historical application:** Entry into the Promised Land and great rejoicing of the people.

● **Future application:** Messianic time or the

millennium of **YAHUSHA**, a thousand-year period in which he reigns with his people.

● **Spiritual application:** Rest in the bosom of **YAHUSHA** and of His kingdom in our lives and hearts; our eternal rest in the lap of our Savior.

Through the **Seven Feast of YAHUAH**, we can clearly see his plan of redemption of all mankind that **YAHUAH** has prepared and in which He commands us to celebrate and learn with earthly things in order to enjoy spiritual things eternally with Him.

If we can see and understand the plan of redemption of **YAHUAH** and make it a reality in our lives, we will see an approach with **YAHUAH** in our personal reality. Only those who are celebrating the feasts of **YAHUAH** will be alert and on guard waiting for the coming of **YAHUSHA**. The feasts are a constant reminder that we must be prepared every year for His coming.

When his feasts are present in our lives, we will long for the arrival of the moment of celebration of the feasts, we will be prepared and we will listen to the trumpet that announces the coming of our Savior **YAHUSHA**.

At the beginning of the year, we remember the redemptive sacrifice of **YAHUSHA** and his resurrection in the feast of Pesach and Matstsah; then we begin to count 50 days to celebrate the advent of the Ruach of **ELOHIYM** in the feast of Pentecost, and as if this were not enough, we prepare to blow the trumpets announcing his second coming. While we are remembering the Second Coming of our Savior, we take the moment to renew our covenant and relationship with **YAHUSHA** on the Day of Atonement and we prepare at the same time to enter the tabernacle of our Creator **YAHUAH** and to reign with our Savior **YAHUSHA** in the kingdom of the millennium.

It is obvious that the master plan of **YAHUAH** is infallible and those who listen and obey His commandments, statutes and precepts, and also keep or celebrate His feasts, will always be alert. By making these holidays a reality in our lives, we are making the redemption plan of **YAHUAH** be more and more clear and true in our hearts. We will always have His master plan present in our lives, consequently, we are alert and prepared for His return. **HâlalYÂH.**

The Seven Feasts of YAHUAH in 2022.

These are the 7 most important Biblical holidays and the ones we should remember while we have life or while we are still alive. They bring us the joy and enjoyment of **YAHUAH** to our lives and those of family and friends. The idea behind these holidays is great joy so that we always remember and have reasons to rejoice in **YAHUAH**.

Here I leave you a table with the names of the 7 Biblical holidays and the days when they fall in the year 2024 in the Gregorian calendar.

1	Passover Dinner / First Shabbath of Unleavened Bread. Exo. 12	April 2
2	The Second Shabbath of Unleavened Bread. Exo. 12 & Lev. 23	April 9
3	Feast of Pentecost (Feast of Weeks) Lev. 23:9-16 Exo. 34:22	May 26
4	Feast of Trumpets Exo. 23:15-16; Deut. 16:16 Lev. 23:23-25. Num. 29:1-6	September 16
5	Day of Atonement (Yom Kippur) Lev. 23:27 - Fasting, prayer, reading the word and repentance.	September 26
6	Feast of Tabernacles Lev. 23:34-35	October 1
7	The Feast of the Eighth Day Lev. 23:39	October 8

Seventy Holidays or Biblical celebration per year.

Recounting the holidays and feast in the bible we can find 70 days a year.

7 Feasts a year: Pesach, Matstsah, Pentecost, Trumpet, Atonement, Tabernacles, Eighth Day

52 Shabbath a year: Each Saturday is considered a feast, because it is the day of rest established by **YAHUAH** since the very first beginning and it is an ordinance FOREVER.

11 blessings at the beginning of each month:

We will find in the bible numerous verses speaking about the blessings or celebration of the first day of each month; sadly to say, it was fraudulently changed by a wrong translation. Instead of using the correct term for the translation of the Hebrew word "chôdesh", which is **MONTH**; in most of the translation has been replaced wrongly by the word "moon". By doing this, they were able to conceal a normal biblical practice of blessing the month at the beginning of each month. However, we have finally restored the translation of the bible to its correct meaning.

Feel free to read these verses using our restored bible version at https://www.YAHUAHbible.com and you will see the correct meaning.

"1 Shemûêl 20:5, 18&24, 2 Melāk̲īm 4:23, Tehīllīm 81:3, Yeshayâhû 66:23". These are only a few verses.

It is very important to understand that these eleven events are not feast nor Shabbath in the bible, these are a celebration presenting each month to **YAHUAH**. There are 11 because the feast of trumpets always starts the first day of the seven month, therefore, the blessings for the new month is kept together with the feast of trumpet.

CHAPTER IV

———◆◇◆———

THE HEBREW ALPHABET

I t is essential to know some important things about the Hebrew alphabet as this will help us to understand the explanations and instructions found in this study. First of all, let's remember that Hebrew was the original language of **YAHUAH**, the language of the Bible and of the people of Yâshârêl, which indicates to us that Hebrew takes us to the origin of everything we know and know.

Lyrics	Name			
א	ב	ג	ד	ה
Alef (silent)	Bet	Gimel (guimel)	Dalet	He (heh)
ו	ז	ח	ט,	י

Waw (au)	Zayin	Cheth	Thet	Yod (yad)
ך כ	ל	ם מ	ן ו	ס
Kaf	Lamed	Mem	Nun	Sa-mech
ע	ף פ	ץ צ	ק	ר
Ayin	Ep	Tsade	Kof	Resh
	ש	ת		
	Shin	Taw		

Important notes about the Alphabet:

Hebrew has no letter J

The letter J has been around for about 500 years. In fact, in the King James Version of the Bible dating back to the year 1611, the J does not appear because it did not exist yet.

Let's remember that the letter J did not exist in most of the languages, including Hebrew, Latin, English, Spanish, German and many more languages.

Hebrew has no letter V

Originally there was only the sound of waw (u), however, the Ashkenazi Yahudiys (Pharisees and scribes) created their own version and inserted, or changed, the pronunciation of waw (u) to v. what we know today as the v sound, was really the w or u sound. In fact, even today the latter v is pronounced as "u or w".

The goal of sharing the Hebrew alphabet is for us to better understand why we are using the correct names of our Creator **YAHUAH** and Salvador **YAHUSHA**.

CHAPTER V

———◆◇◆———

THE NAME OF YAHUAH (יהוה)

O ver the years we have been told many uncertain things about what the correct name of our Creator is; all those names that are circulating and proclaiming in the podiums were misrepresented and none of them is the real name. His real name is **YAHUAH** (יהוה). These four letters in Hebrew are the ones used for the name of **YAHUAH**, which have been misinterpreted and therefore obscured the true name of our Creator. This is the reading of the name of our **ELOHIYM**.

Y	Y		י

AH	He (*at the beginning of a word it is read as He, but in the middle, alone or at the end it is read as AH. The h sounds like the English H, but stronger, it is not mute*)	ה
U	Waw (*represents the vowel U*)	ו
AH	He(*at the beginning of a word it is read as He, but in the middle, alone or at the end it is read as AH. The h sounds like the English H, but stronger, it is not mute*)	ה

You don't need to be a scientist to read these acronyms, much less to put them together and correctly read the name of **YAHUAH**. The letters are 1. **Y** 2. **AH** 3. **U** 4. **AH**. If we put them together, we will get the name of our Creator **YAHUAH**. Do not forget that the H is not mute, but in the Hebrew language it sounds when it is at the beginning and when it is in the middle of a word. However, if it is located at the end, it tends to be mute.

Who changed His name in the Bible?

The Yahudiy called Ashkenazis or Pharisees (scribes) created the dogma or superstition that the Name of **YAHUAH** it was too sacred to pronounce, and then they fraudulently decided to stop articulating

His name. Even the Ashkenazi or Yahudiy Pharisees (scribes) themselves decided to use the title of Adonay, which means Lord, instead of the name of **YAHUAH.** Despite the fact that in the writing of the original Hebrew it is still intact, they decided to pronounce it as Adonay and thus created that tradition and fulfilled the prophecies that say that, over time and by sinning with pagan gods, they would forget His real name: **YAHUAH.**

After the destruction of the temple in Yerûshâlaim, the name was forgotten. However, it still appeared in the Hebrew Scriptures. Despite this, at the time of translating the texts, Rome paid its translators to remove the name of **YAHUAH** of the Bible and to have it replaced by the title of Lord (or Baal). It is important to note that this title is not only applied to anyone, but also comes from the name of Baal, a pagan god hated by **YAHUAH.**

This is how the name of **YAHUAH** was replaced in the Bible by the name of Baal or Lord. Although it has always been present in the original Hebrew text, the name of **YAHUAH** was removed from the Bible about 7 thousand times. In translations into other languages, the name of **YAHUAH** has been DELETED.

Finally, we must not forget that **YAHUAH,** as the **ELOHIYM** of the Yâshârêl, was hated by the Greeks and the Romans, so they tried to erase his name from the Bible when Constantine united the church and the state.

The name of Yah (יה)

First of all, it is important to remember that the name of **YAHUAH** He has a short version, that is, His name has 4 letters, but the short version consists only of the first two letters.

The short version of His name is **YAHU** or **YAH** (יה)

Y	Y	י
AH	He(*at the beginning of a word it is read as He, but in the middle, alone or at the end it is read as AH. The h sounds like the English H, but stronger, it is not mute*)	ה

Normally, we say **YAH** or **YAHU** which is the way the short version of the name of **YAHUAH**. This reduced version is the one used in the names of the prophets and servants of **YAHUAH**. They show how their names are part of the Creator. For example: Eli*YAHU* or Eli*YAH* (Elias) - Yirme*YAHU* or Yirme*YAH* (Yirmeyâhû) - Yesha*YAHU* or Yesha*YAH* (Isaiah).

This short version appears about 50 times in the Bible, by itself referring to **YAHUAH** and countless times in combination with names of other Bible characters.

Is the name of YAHUAH in the Bible?

Of course it is, it has always been and it will always be, about 7 thousand times. Just look at the Bible in Hebrew and you will realize that his name is there. You can also look at the translation of your Bible and you will see that where they have put the title of Lord with a capital letter and in some cases in all capital letters they are replacing the name of **YAHUAH.** They also use the term Elohiym so as not to propagate the true name of **YAHUAH.** This means that YES, the name of **YAHUAH** it is still intact in the original language (Hebrew); only in the translations have they hidden it. However, in the last times and according to the prophecies, His name **"YAHUAH"** will be known all over the world as it will be restored. That is what we are doing today, restoring the true name of our Creator **YAHUAH**.

It is curious to be able to find in the translation of the Bible into Swahili, the transliteration of the true name of our Creator **YAHUAH**. Logical, after the revisions of this Bible, they changed the name of our Creator.

Why is it important to know the name of YAHUAH?

Don't you think that knowing the true name of our Creator is an important fact? We as humans go to certain extremes just to have our name recognized. In fact, when we are called by another name we even get angry and argue, because it is important that others know our name correctly since it is our unique identity and what distinguishes us from others. If your name is Peter and you hear someone calling Paul, it is logical that you do not turn to see because it is not your name. But if you hear someone saying, "Peter, Peter"... you will immediately turn around and pay attention, because you know that is your name.

How much more important then is the name of the Creator of the universe and of everything that exists. If **YAHUAH** wouldn't want us to know his real name and pronounce it correctly *why then the name of* **YAHUAH** *is present about 7 thousand times in the Old Testament?* Our Creator is known by many names, but only ONE is His true name and by which He alone is called. Nothing and no one else in heaven, on earth or under the earth has that name because it is reserved SOLELY and exclusively for **YAHUAH**.

John 14:13 *And all that you will ask of the Father* **(YAHUAH)** *in my name* **(YAHUSHA)**, *I will do it, so that the Father* **(YAHUAH)** *be glorified in the Son* **(YAHUSHA)**.

So, if we ask for something to **YAHUAH** in the name of **YAHUSHA,** we will receive it. *But how are we going to receive something if we don't even know whom we are asking, much less on whose behalf we are asking for it?* This is the main reason why we always ask and ask, but never receive: we don't know how to ask and we don't ask correctly.

If we meet someone on the street and he says to us: "Peter, give me something to eat for I have nothing to eat" the first thing we do is tell him: "My name is not Peter, my name is (for example) James." And if we are in a good mood and we feel merciful, then we decide to give him something, we do not give him much because he is not addressing us correctly, instead he is thinking that we are someone else. However, we give him something out of our humbly heart.

Now, if we meet someone who calls us by our name, the first thing that happens is that we show our amazement. Then, because he calls us by our name, we give him what he asks for and much more, because we are glad that such a person recognizes us and calls us by our name. Consequently, we overflow into giveaways.

Think about those two scenarios and then get on the feet of **YAHUAH;** you will be able to understand better what I am saying. It is of the utmost importance that we know His real name **YAHUAH** and the name of his son **YAHUSHA**.

Other names of YAHUAH in the Bible

The Bible records other names that have been used since the beginning of time to refer to **YAHUAH**. These can be titles to refer to Him by some specific situation or to allude to a certain experience of one of the biblical characters.

Ĕlôhıym (אֱלֹהִים): It is the first name that appears in the Bible, in **Berēshıth 1**:[1] *In the beginning Ĕlôhıym created the heavens and the earth.* It is essential to mention that this term appears about 2,601 times in the Old Testament and that it is used to refer to the Creator **YAHUAH** and also to other pagan gods, idols or deities. On the other hand, it is also important to emphasize that the term "**Ĕlôhıym**" is in the plural, that is, it means "gods".

Êl (אֵל): Means the "All-Powerful One" and appears about 242 times in the OT. **Berēshīṯh 35**: [1] ...*make an altar there to the Êl who appeared to you when you were running away from your brother Êśâw.*

ĔLÔAHH (אֱלוֹהַ): Singular form of **Ĕlôhıym** and appears about 57 times in the A.T. **Debārīm 32**: [15] *... Then he abandoned **ĔLÔAHH** which made him...*

ĔLÂHH (אֱלָה): Appears about 95 times in the A.T. **Daniel 2**: [23] *...To you, oh **ĔLâhh** of my fathers...*

In short, there are many combinations that use the names mentioned above and that lead to a countless number of names. However, the proper or main name is **YAHUAH**.

Titles, attributes and combinations of the names of YAHUAH

As mentioned above, in addition to the main names of **YAHUAH**, there are also titles, attributes and combinations according to a specific situation or circumstance.

Combinations with Êl (אֵל):

● **Êl Elyôn** (עֶלְיוֹן)- The Most High. **Berēshīṯh 14**: [18] *And **Malkîy-Tsedeq** king of **Shâlêm** brought forth bread and wine: and he was the **Kôhên** of the most **Elyôn Êl.***

● **Êl Rŏıy** (רְאִי) - The one who sees. **Berēshı̄th 16**: [13] *And she called the name of* **YAHUAH** *(יהוה) that spoke unto her, You* **ÊL Rŏîy**: *for she said, Have I also here looked after him that sees me?*

● **Êl Shadday** (שַׁדַּי) - The Almighty. **Berēshı̄th 17**: [1] *And when Abrâm was ninety years old and nine,* **YAHUAH** *appeared to Abrâm, and said unto him, I am* **SHADDAY EL**; *walk before me, and be you perfect."*

● **Êl Ôlâm** (עוֹלָם) - The Eternal. **Berēshı̄th 21**:[33] *And Abrâhâm planted a grove in Beêr Sheba, and called there on the name of* **YAHUAH**, *the* **OLAM ÊL**.

● **Êl Ĕlôhêy Yasharêl** (אֵל אֱלֹהֵי יִשְׂרָאֵל) – **Êl of Yâshârêl**. **Berēshı̄th 33**: [20] *And he erected there an altar, and called it* **Êl Ĕlôhêy -Yâshârêl**.

Combinations with YAHUAH (יְהֹוָה):

● **YAHUAH Yireh** (יְהֹוָה יִרְאֶה)- YAHUAH Will Provide. **Berēshı̄th 22**: [14] *And Abrâhâm called the name of that place* **YAHUAH YIR'EH**: *as it is said to this day, In the mount of* **YAHUAH**, *it shall be seen.*

● **YAHUAH Nissıy** (יְהֹוָה נִסִּי) - YAHUAH is my banner. **Šhemōth 17**:[15] **And Môsheh built an altar, and called the name of it** YAHUAH Nissîy.

● **YAHUAH Shâlôm** (יְהֹוָה שָׁלוֹם) - YAHUAH is peace. **Šhōphṭı̄m 6**:[24] *Then Gidŏn built an altar there unto* **YAHUAH**, *and called it* **YAHUAH Shâlôm**: *unto this day it is yet in Ophrâh of the Ăbîy Hâezrîy.*

● **YAHUAH Tsâbâ (צְבָא)** - **YAHUAH** of the Armies. *1 Shemûêl 1:*[3] *And this man went up out of his city yearly to worship and to sacrifice unto YAHUAH Tsâbâ in Shîylôh. And the two sons of Êlîy, Chophnîy and Pîynechâs, the kôhên of YAHUAH, were there.*

● **YAHUAH Tsedek (צֶדֶק)** - **YAHUAH** is our righteousness. *Jeremias 23:* [6] *In his days Yahûdâh shall be saved, and Yâshârêl shall dwell safely: and this is his name whereby he shall be called, YAHUAH Our TSEDEQ.*

● **YAHUAH Shâm (שָׁם)** - **YAHUAH** is right there. **Yechezqêl 48***:* [35] *It was round about eighteen thousand measures: and the name of the city from that day shall be, YAHUAH SHÂM.*

● **YAHUAH Qâdash (קָדַשׁ)** – **YAHUAH** sanctifies. *Šhemōṯh 31:* [13] *Speak you also unto the children of Yâshârêl, saying, verily my Shabbâth you shall keep: for it is a sign between me and you throughout your generations; that you may know that I am YAHUAH Qâdash that does sanctify you.*

● **YAHUAH Râphâ (רְפָא)** - **YAHUAH** heals. **Šhemōṯh 15**: [26] *And said, If you will diligently hearken to the voice of YAHUAH your ÊLÔHÎYM, and will do that which is right in his sight, and will give ear to his commandments, and keep all his statutes, I will put none of these diseases upon you, which I have brought upon the Mitsrayim: for I am YAHUAH Râphâ.*

● **YAHUAH Rââh (רָעָה)** – **YAHUAH** is my shepherd. **Tehīllīm 23:** [2] *YAHUAH is my Rââh; I shall not want.*

THE NAME OF YAHUAH (הוהי)

Other Attributes and Titles of YAHUAH

● **Ădônây (אֲדֹנָי)** - Sir, lord, master. **Berēshīṯh 15**: *[2] And Abrâm said, ĂDÔNÂY YAHUAH, what will you give me, seeing I go childless, and the steward of my house is this Ĕlîyezer of Dammeśeq?*

● **Qâdôsh Yasharêl (יִשְׂרָאֵל)** - Holy one of Yâshârêl. **Yeshayâhû 1**:[4] *Ah sinful nation, a people laden with iniquity, a seed of evildoers, children that are corrupters: they have forsaken YAHUAH, they have provoked the QÂDÔSH of Yâshârêl unto anger, they are gone away backward.*

● **Hâyâh (הָיָה) Âshêr (אֲשֶׁר) Hâyâh (הָיָה)** – I AM WHO I AM. **Shemōṯh 3**:[14] *And ĔLÔHÎYM said unto Môsheh, HAYAH ÂSHÊR HAYAH: and he said, Thus shall you say unto the children of Yâshârêl, HAYAH has sent me unto you.*

What is the origin of the word lord?

The word **lord** it comes from the Hebrew term Baal which refers to a Semitic deity or god who was hated by **YAHUAH** and who was the cause of all the pains of the people of **YAHUAH** or Yâshârêl. The word Baal means *sir, master or owner.* It is good to remember that the full name is Baalzebub (Beelzebub or Beelzebub), which translated means "lord of the Flies». It is the same term used in some parts of the New Testament, in *Matthew 10:25, Matthew 12:24, Mark 3:22*, to refer to the prince of demons.

This means that we have been taught to use the term or title of lord to refer to our Creator **YAHUAH** or to our Savior **YAHUSHA.** As a consequence, they completely deceived us as they lead us to use pagan terms and abhorred by **YAHUAH**. Instead of calling our Creator **YAHUAH** by his name or to our Savior **YAHUSHA** we are constantly invoking the name of Baal or the prince of demons. Do you think that **YAHUAH** like to be confused with a pagan and hateful god?

Šhemōṯh 20: *³ You shall have no other gods before me. ⁴ You shall not make unto you any graven image, or any likeness of anything that is in heaven above, or that is in the earth beneath, or that is in the water under the earth. ⁵ You shall not bow down yourself to them, nor serve them: for I **YAHUAH** your **ĔLÔHÎYM** am a jealous **ÊL,** visiting the iniquity of the fathers upon the children unto the third and fourth generation of them that hate me; ⁶ And showing mercy unto thousands of them that love me, and keep my commandments.*

Where does the word God come from?

The word "god[1]" it comes straight from the Latin **deus**, 'deity, god'. The Latin term derives in turn from the Indo-European "deiwos", from the root "deiw", 'to shine, to be white', from which the Greek term also derives **Ζεύς (Zeus).** In fact, the Spanish word "dios" is identical in pronunciation to the Greek **Διός**

1

(Elohiym), the genitive form of *Zeus[2]* (the main god of Greek mythology, father of the "theos", which are the minor gods). Wikipedia

As you can see, there is a similarity or equality between the Latin terms deus and Zeus (god of Greek mythology). Since childhood we have been taught that we should call our Creator **YAHUAH**, God, or to our Savior **YAHUSHA**, Lord. However, this teaching leads us to names of pagan or mythological deities or gods. It is for this reason that I try not to include the word god in my vocabulary and prefer to use the Biblical term ***ELOHIYM***, which literally means gods in a general term and also refers to our Creator **YAHUAH ELOHIYM**. In fact, when we look at the word ELOHIYM in the Bible, the original Hebrew term is, in the vast majority of cases, gods in plural.

Berēshīṯh 1:[2] *In the beginning **ELOHIYM** created the heavens and the earth.* The original Hebrew term used in the Bible is **ELOHIYM**.

This information is highly sensitive and many will not accept or assimilate it, but for those who are called from and by **YAHUAH,** they will be interested and will seek to know the truth of His name.

The Name of YAHUSHA
(יוהשע)

I know that for some this will be a hard drink to assimilate and a hard truth to accept, however, the truth is the truth and does not need to be defended. Those who are of the truth will sooner or later accept

2

it. Anyway, I fully understand how difficult it can be for many to hear these words when we have been taught the opposite since childhood; it is very difficult to change habits that have been passed down from generation to generation. Therefore, I always ask my readers to do their own research and in the end they will come to the same conclusions. All the information presented here has its supporting source that you can read whenever you want. Nothing is of private interpretation, on the contrary, it is of common interpretation for all humanity.

His son's name is **YAHUSHA** (**יוהשע**)

The name of our Savior always bears the name of His Father **YAHUAH**, and this is why his name is **YAHU** (short version of the Father's name) and **SHA**.

His name means *I AM the one who comes, defends, liberates, helps, preserves, rescues, saves, brings salvation, your Savior and the one who leads you to victory*. That's **YAHUSHA**, the Son.

Y	Y	י
AH	He(*at the beginning of a word it is read as He, but in the middle, alone or at the end it is read as AH. The h sounds like the English H, it is not mute*)	ה
U	Waw/U	ו

SH	Sh	שׁ
A	Ayin	ע

As you can see, the first two letters are the same ones contained in the Father's name **YAHUAH**, I mean, **YAHU**, as I explained earlier. This is the perfect name that represents the Son **YAHUSHA** as part of the Father **YAHUAH**.

The origin of the Name of Jesus

*If there was not the **J**, then where does the name Jesus come from[3]?*

As we explained above and as I think you all already understand the point, let's consider the importance of a name. A person's name is very important, so much so that **YAHUAH,** although some try to hide it, he has always used his real name throughout history, that is, **YAHUAH.** In the same way, he has shown his name through the names of many prophets and chosen of **YAHUAH**. It is so deeply important that it even goes so far as to change the name of many characters in the Bible, for example, "Jacob "Yaăqôb - Yâshârêl", Abram–"Abrâhâm". These are just a few examples so that we remember that **YAHUAH** tends

3

to change people's names because of their relevance.

Do you think that **YAHUAH** *told Yôsêph and* Miryâm *(Mary) to name His Only Son a Greek or Latin name?* Such a theory is impossible and unthinkable. What we have been led to believe is that our Savior does not bear a Hebrew name, but a pagan name. IMPOSSIBLE. The name of Jesus comes from the Greek "Ιησούς" which is read Iesus, since the J did not exist in any of the languages. In turn it comes from the Latin "Iesus" which is read as it is written.

Once again I remind you that the J did not exist neither in Hebrew, nor in Greek, nor in Latin nor in any other language, not even in English. While we have already learned about the name Zeus, we have not yet learned the similarity and meaning of the name "Iesus". This name literally means:

Ie: hail (when the person bows down or salutes a king or ruler)

Sus: It is the pronunciation of the name Zeus in English and in other languages.

So the name means *"hail Zeus"*, a phrase referring to an acclamation of the pagan and mythological Greek god, who also, given the meaning of the name, is known as the sun god.

Do you think that everything that our Savior did for us on the Calvary should be given and credited to the pagan gods created by man? Or how would one feel about creating or doing something wonderful and another is the one who takes credit for that work that you made or performed? I personally would feel bereft, disappointed and even angry. But we have done the same with our Savior **YAHUSHA**. We have stripped him of his works, miracles and vicarious death for us when we attribute his works to the god created (Jesus) by Constantine and the Roman Empire.

CHAPTER VI

---❖---

CONSTANTINE AND THE
COUNCIL OF NICAEA

Around 325 AD, the Council of Nicaea met and the first ecumenical meeting was held; there were leaders of all the major sects and religions of that time. Emperor Constantine united all these groups in order to create union and define the new god who would rule not only his empire, but all the religions and empires of the world. Constantine gathered 1,780 leaders and of those he chose 144 spokesmen. He divided the rest into groups of 12 and designated a good number of them as *scribes and translators*.

However, thanks to their appearance as Yâshârêl, some were rejected and banned from the council. As a result, there was not a single Yâshârêl, much less a Levite, present at that meeting. That is, there was no guardian of the word of **YAHUAH** present. These religious leaders had to decide which would be the only god they would worship and which would be the deity of the Roman Empire or of Constantine. The names of more than 50 gods were chosen to select the only god of Constantine's empire. However, the religious and ecumenical leaders could not reach any agreement because everyone had their own personal interests. This is a list of the main gods who were competing to become the only god of Constantine's empire.

Jove[4] (Zeus), Jupiter (Roman version of Zeus), Salenus, Baal, Thor, Gade, Apollo, Juno, Aries, Taurus, Minerva, Rhets, Mithra, Theo, Fragapatti, Atys, Durga, Indra, Neptune, Vulcan, *Kriste* (ancient Germanic gofd or Hindu *krishna* god), Agni, Croesus, Pelides, Huit, Hermes, Thulis, Thammus, Eguptus, Iao, ... , Saturn, Gitchens, Minos, Maximus, Hecla, and Phernes.[5]

Then, they created raffles to reduce the number of the gods and thus reach the one they needed. The number of gods was gradually reduced to 21 candidate gods for the position.

The god of Constantine's Empire

A year and 5 months later they still hadn't decided which one would be the god of the empire; but they had managed to reduce the list of the gods to 5:

● Jove (Greek Zeus or Roman Jupiter)

4
5

- Kriste (ancient Germanic god or Krishna, Hindu god)
- Mars (Mars, god of war, Italic god)
- Crite (Caesar or Crite of the Chaldeans, ancient god)
- Siva (Shiva, Hindu god).

The new empire had the imperative need to create their own god, since they did not accept or worship the ELOHIYM (God) of the Yâshârêl; that is why they did not let a single Yâshârêl participate in their council. In the end they managed to decide by signs and the winning god was Kriste (ancient Germanic god or Hindu god Krishna) whom they declared as the god of all nations and the earth. They also agreed to reject any god other than Krishna or, better pronounced in Latin since it was the dominant language, Christ.

This decision would reverberate for all the centuries to come. He would unleash the nine crusades (supposed holy wars) and other crusades in different territories and the inquisition or holy inquisition against the supposed heresy that was punished with the death penalty (according to Rome or the Catholic church at that time).

Matthew 24: *²² If those days were not shortened,* **no one would be saved**, *but they will be shortened because of **the chosen ones**. ²³ So, if someone says to you, "Look, here is the Mâshîyach (**YAHUSHA**)", or "Look, there he is", don't believe it. ²⁴ For false Mâshîyach and false prophets will arise and perform great signs and wonders, so that, if possible,* **they will deceive even the elect.**

This is exactly what they created: a false messiah for the purpose of alienating humanity from the true Mâshîyach **(YAHUSHA)**. The deception is such that even the elect could be deceived, just as **Matthew** says.

Remember that among those present at that council were the Pharisees or Ashkenazi[6], who have always been public enemy number one of **YAHUAH** and of his teachings. So much so that they were the forerunner force in the death sentence of **YAHUSHA**, the same ones that **YAHUSHA** called them "white sepulchers."

Matthew 23: *[27] Woe unto you, scribes and Pharisees, hypocrites! for you are like unto whited sepulchers, which indeed appear beautiful outward, but are within full of dead men's bones, and of all uncleanness. [28] Even so you also outwardly appear righteous unto men, but within you are full of hypocrisy and iniquity.*

Human representative of the god for the Empire of Constantine

However, they were not finished yet. They still needed to choose who would be the representative of the created god of the empire of Constantine on earth, that is, his mortal, human representative.

These were the main names of the men who were appointed to the position of mortal representative of the new god of the empire that the Pharisees,

---

6

scribes and ecumenical leaders proposed as their representative on earth.

Zarathustra, Thothma, Abrâhâm, Brahma, Atys, Thammus, Joshu, Sakaya, Habron, Bali, Crite, Chrisna, Thulis, Wittoba and Speio. In addition to a list of forty-six names.

For twelve months they argued without being able to reach an agreement on who would be the mortal representative.

So the Emperor Constantine concluded that the gods would not let them choose another man and at that moment they agreed in the name of Iesu (Iesus, jesus) or hesus[7] (esus) *gallo-Celtic god better known as lord.* Thus they created a combination of worship: *Ie means hail and his version of Zeus*; or *hail hesus,* so they created the moral representative praising the god of mythology and using the Latin version or combination of the name "Jesus". They decided then to change and update all the books and texts with the new name. You can read this information in the hidden book of Eskra[8]. On the other hand, they also decided to change all the names with Y and establish the J as part of the alphabet. Some names are:

Iesus (jesus), Iupiter (jupiter) Iune (juno – June).
So the new god of the empire had been created:
Iesus Kriste   Hesus Krishna
Jesus Christ   Jesus Christ

John 5:43 *I- (**YAHUSHA**) I have come in the name of my Father (**YAHUAH**), and you do not receive*

7
8

me; if another comes in his own name, him you will receive. These are the literal words of our Savior **YAHUSHA** where he tells us the harsh truth: the one whom the world received and accepted is the savior created by men and not the true **YAHUSHA**.

In conclusion, Constantine and the council of Nicaea created the god they wanted for the Roman Empire and the god that the following generations would worship, the same god that all of us were taught to worship since childhood. They decided to change the truth and disguise it for their own personal and empire benefits. As a result, all generations from that time to the present day are still under the spell of Constantine and his leaders.

That is to say that when we sing, pray, praise and use the titles given by the decree and teaching of the Emperor Constantine; we are giving our prayers and praises to their gods thinking that it is to our Creator.

Many say, **YAHUAH** knows my heart and that's what matters. Yes of course that **YAHUAH** knows the heart of each one and that is why we ask of Him and we do not receive everything we ask for. **Matthew 7**:23 *And then will I profess unto them, I never knew you: depart from me, you that work iniquity.*

Those believing and saying to themselves "he knows my heart"; sadly to say but that is why he will answer you all "I never knew you, depart from me..."

Remember the example I told you; if someone calls you by another name, do you respond? Let's be realistic and sincere and let's stop making so many excuses that only lead to perdition.

At the end of the day, who are you crying out to? Or do you cry out to the true Creator **YAHUAH ELOHIYM** or you cry out to the deities or names created by man. Do not forget, it is your decision and only you are responsible for your actions. No one will give an account or excuses for you. This is only for the ones who believe in **YAHUSHA**.

CHAPTER VII

THE FIRST BIBLES

The controversies, revolts and divisions created in that year lasted from 325 AD to 500 and both AD. We must remember that the Bible had not yet been translated into other languages, much less into English. At that time there was the Septuagint or LXX[9], a Greek version translated by the Ptolemies (285 – 246 AD). It was then, around the year 328 AD, that St. Geronimo translated the Vulgate Bible[10] from Greek (LXX) to Latin, and used the new name of the ELOHIYM created for the world and mankind by Constantine and the council of Nicaea.

The first English bible written by hand was by John Wycliffe, 1380. It was translated out of the Latin Vulgate, which was the only source text available to Wycliffe. The Pope at that time was so infuriated by his teachings and his translation of the Bible

---

9
10

into English that 44 years after Wycliffe had died, he ordered the bones to be dug-up, crushed, and scattered in the river! Yet the church still threatened to kill anyone who read the scripture in any language other than Latin... even when they knew that Latin was not an original language of the scriptures.

In 1535 Myles Coverdale printed the first complete Bible in the English, using the German texts and Latin sources of Martin Luther. On October 4, 1535, the Coverdale Bible was published. Later in the church of Switzerland a group of theologians gather to create the Geneva Bible, published 1560.

When Prince James VI of Scotland became **King James I of England**, the Protestant clergy approached the new King in 1604, because they wanted a new bible version instead of the Geneva Bible. They did not want the controversial marginal notes (proclaiming the Pope an Anti-Christ). Essentially the leaders of the church desired a Bible for the people. This translation was the result of the combined effort of about fifty scholars using: The Tyndale New Testament, The Coverdale Bible, The Matthews Bible, The Great Bible, The Geneva Bible, and even the Rheims New Testament. In 1611 King James Bible came into the public available to everyone.

It should be noted that all these versions of the Bible were already impregnated or filled with the decisions made by the Council of Nicaea and their god created by them since all the translations came from the Latin Vulgate version or the LXX version of the Greek. None of these versions were based directly on the truth of the Hebrew text.

This is how all mankind knows the version created by Constantine and his regents. Remember that at that time it was not allowed to read the Bible or share it because it was the privilege of a few (the religious leaders of the Roman Empire and the church–state merger created by Constantine). In other words, the Catholic Church controlled everything under the rule of Constantine.

However, despite all these attempts, the original Hebrew text was preserved intact for centuries and years to come. They could only change the translated versions, but never the original text with the ordinances of **YAHUAH** and His word given to His people.

These data are available to anyone who wants and wishes to search for the truth. However, the truth is not for everyone; it is easier to live in deception and lies than to be free and know the truth.

John 8: *32 and you will know the truth, and the truth will set you free.*

As we can see from the story and which you can read for yourselves in the links at the footer, the god created by humans or the names given to that god are not the correct name of our Savior or Redeemer. That is not the name of our Savior, the name of our Savior bears the name of the Father **YAHUAH** and it is in Hebrew, it is neither Greek, nor Latin, nor Hispanic nor English, nor of any other race. His real name is **YAHUSHA**.

This is the reason why several years ago, we started a very interesting project. We decided that was about time that we have His name restored in every places of the Bible. Therefore, we have been restoring His name throughout all the passages taking them directly from the original Hebrew texts.

We also decided to restore every single name in the bible, because names are so important that changing them will affect the correct meaning of them. We are restoring all proper names (places, cities, towns,) and we have been restoring many bible verses that have been wrongly translated, including restoring entire sections that were deleted from the translated versions.

We are expecting to have all 66 books of the bible restored by 2025 and then, we will start another round of restoration, but this time, creating real bible comments with no bias so we all get to know the truth. We will be also restoring other inspired books of the bible that were left or hidden to us under false excuses; books such as Jubilees, Enoch and many more. Visit https://www.yahuahbible.com

CHAPTER VIII

DIFFERENT TYPES OF CALENDARS

Let's look at some important facts about the different types of calendars that have been the guide or compass used by mankind to determine certain times, solemn dates and holidays. Some calendars were based on what was observed in the stars, the sky, and the position of the planets, the moon and the sun. This is where the different types of calendars come from:

Moon: The rotation of the moon is used as a basis for measuring the months of the year.

Moon-sun: Created by the Sumerians or Babylonians, Mesopotamia and the Middle East. As they had to take into account the weather for crops and agriculture, they also had to observe the seasons.

Sun: Created by the Mitsrayimians, who understood that a year lasted 365 days and divided the months into 30 days (12 x 30 = 360 days). Since the count was not enough to reach the 365 days, they used the remaining 5 days for holidays or solemn days[11]. They looked directly at the sun as the main star, Amun-Ra[12] as the sun god and supreme deity of Mitsrayim. His calendar was based on the movement of the sun.[13]

Here are some important notes about calendars that we should consider before talking about the biblical calendar.

Chinese Calendar[14]

Each year is made up of 12 months and, every three years, an extra month is added to level the gap. The date on which the new Year is celebrated is always different, since it moves to the day on which the first full moon occurs, that is, between our January 21 and February 21.

Chinese New Year is celebrated on the second New Moon, after the winter solstice and following a legend where Buddha and 12 animals, which correspond to the Chinese zodiac signs, they are the protagonists. The animals are as follows: the rat, the ox, the tiger, the rabbit, the dragon, the snake, the horse, the goat, the monkey, the rooster, the dog and the pig.

Islamic Calendar

Islam also has its own calendar, and the year is

11
12
13
14

slightly shorter than ours - 364 days, divided into 12 months. This calendar is based on the lunar movement; each month begins the day after a new moon night.

The Islamic lunar year has between 354 and 355 days which are divided into months of 29 or 30 days. The days take their name from their numerical order: Sunday is the first day and Saturday is the seventh and last. The exception is on Friday, which takes its name from the midday prayer, when the entire Islamic community tries to gather.

Hindu Calendar

This is governed by both solar and lunar principles, which gives way to 12 months that are guided by the moon and have between 29 and 30 days each. In addition, every three years, an extra month is added.

The Indian year is divided into 6 seasons, one season every two months: Vesanta (spring), Grichma (summer), Varea (rains), Sarad (autumn), Hemanta (winter), Sis (dew).

In India, New Year's Day is celebrated around April 15, when it is commemorated when, according to them and in their superstition, Bramha created the Universe. This means that the Hindu year begins in spring.

The Hebrew Calendar

This calendar consists of 12 months, although there are leap years that last 13 months and occur every

3 years.

The Hebrew calendar combines between the solar year and the lunar month. For this reason, the days begin at the beginning of the night, which is why the beginning of the months is marked by the new moon and the harvest cycles.

The Yahudiy's New Year coincides with the beginning of the economic year in Southwest Asia and Northeast Africa, marking the beginning of the agricultural cycle.

The names of the Hebrew months have their origin in ancient Babylon, where they were adopted by the Yahudiy exiled by King Nebuchadnezzar II, an exile that lasted 70 years (586 BC). C. - 516 a. C). In the past, the months were named only by their numerical order, starting in the spring with the first month, Âbîyb (Nisan). But in the times of the New Testament there was a second calendar of civil or official use that began with the month of Tisri, whose first day was the civil New Year or Rosh Hashanah, which continues in force to this day. It should be noted that the Hebrew calendar is not the biblical calendar.

This is the calendar with the names of the months in Hebrew and the month, or months that corresponds in the Gregorian calendar, that is, the calendar used in the world today. You will see that every Biblical or Hebrew month falls in two months of the Gregorian calendar; this is because the Biblical month falls in most cases in the middle of the month in the Gregorian calendar, thus always occupying two months.

Mention of the month in the Bible.	Name of the Month	According to the Gregorian calendar	Months of the Holidays
Šhemōṯh 12:2-37; 13:4; Nehemiah 2:1	Âbîyb	March – April	Passover Unleavened bread
1 Kings 6:1	Iyar or Zif	April – May	
....	Siwan	May – June	Shâbûa – Pentecost
Yechezqêl 8:14	Tammuz	June – July	
...	Ab	July – August	
Nehemiah 6:15	Elul	August – September	Feast of the Trumpets Day of Atonement
1 Kings 8:2	Ethanim or Tishri	September – October	Feast of Tabernacles
1 Kings 6:38	Marcheswan o Bul	October – November	Feast of the Eighth Day - The Great Saturday
Zechariah 7:1	Kislew	November –December	
...	Tewet	December – January	
Zechariah 1:7	Shewat	January – February	
...	Adar	February –March	

Julian Calendar[15]

The Julian calendar was the one used before the Gregorian one. Established in honor of Julius Caesar, it came into operation in 45 BC. He had a year divided into 12 months and, like the Gregorian, he had a leap day in February and every four years.

Anyway, with this one, one day was lost every 129 years, because it did not coincide so much with the solar year. With the Gregorian Reform, this error was corrected and now only one day is lost every 3,000 years.

Roman Calendar

Originally the Roman calendar had 10 months (6 months of 30 days and 4 of 31 days). The beginning of the year was Martius[16] (mars or March), named in commemoration of the god of war.

1. *Martius*: month of Mars (March), god of war, father of Romulus and Remus[17]
2. *Aprilis*: month of opening of flowers.
3. *Maius*[18]: month of Maia (May), goddess of abundance
4. *Junius*[19]: month of Juno, godess of home and family
5. *Quintilis*: fifth month
6. *Sextilis*: sixth month
7. *September*: seventh month
8. *October*: eighth month

15
16
17
18
19

9. *November*: ninth month
10. *December*: tenth month
11. *Januarius*[20]: month of Janus, god of the portals
12. *Februarius*[21]: month of the purification bonfires (February)

It should be noted that the fifth month or Quintilis became Iulius (Julius or July) in commemoration of Julius Caesar[22].

The month Sextilis or sixth became Augustus or August in commemoration of Octavian Augustus[23]

Origin of the Sol Invictus on December 25

The purpose of all these changes was to be able to achieve unification and comply with Constantine's willingness to take the date of the god Mithras, whom he worshipped, or the sun god as a solemn date to be celebrated for centuries to come and idol Tammuz mentioned in the book of Yechezqêl (Ezekiel) and Yirmeyâhû (Jeremiah)

The winter solstice began to be celebrated since prehistoric times in what is now Europe and Asia Minor. And that is why, in many cultures, long before Christianity, the day **25 (of December)** was associated with the birthday of the Sun, with feasts to different deities that inspired various religions. The god Mithras, in Rome, was one of these, also

20
21
22
23

the Sol Invictus, because the cycle of the new year was Christmas or Natalis solis invicti (the Birth of the Undefeated Sun).[24]

As the feast Dies Natalis Solis Invicti was becoming part of the oldest Roman festivals, that is, the Saturnalia, were growing in importance. These festivals were held in honor of Saturn, the god of sowing, and began on December 17 and ended on the 25th of the same month. These were days of joy, exchange of gifts, great banquets, games and the liberation of slaves.

This was how the name of this pagan celebration was changed to the name we know today as Christmas or the supposed birth of the god of Constantine or of the empire. Observing that feast was a mandate, so not celebrating or keeping this pagan feast led, at that time, to persecution and death.

What we have not been told that there is an ancient idol or pagan god behind this celebration, one mentioned in the bible, which is Tammuz. Search for yourself and discover the blatant truth behind this idol, you will be surprised.

The days of the Weeks and their dedication

At the same time (321) and based on the Mesopotamian calendar, the Emperor Constantine also implemented the seven-day week. In addition, he

---

24

decreed that on Sunday (**dies solis, day of the sun**) it was a day of rest to worship the new god. Thus, the Biblical day of rest (Saturday) was fraudulently changed by these people to the one we know today as Sunday or the day of the sun.

Sunday: *dies solis* or the day of the sun (worship of the sun).

Monday: *dies lunae* or the day of the moon (worship of the moon).

Tuesday: *Martis díes* or Mars day (god of war).

Wednesday: *Mercurii díes* o day of Mercury (god of commerce)

Thursday: *dies Iovis* o day of Jupiter (god of Roman mythology, which is equal to Zeus, Greek god)

Friday: *Veneris dies* or day of Venus (goddess of Roman mythology).

Saturday: The English term "Saturday" comes from the biblical Latin *sabbătum*, then from the Greek σάββατον (*sabbaton*), and this one from the Hebrew יום השבת (*shabbath*), which means "rest" or "Shabbath day". The only day to which they could not change the name nor YAHUAH allowed them to desecrate it by changing the name was the Shabbath. This day retains its original name and means rest or Sabbath. In the beginning the days of the week were enumerated as they had no name. The original names are still preserved in the Portuguese language, with the exception that they include the name of Sunday. But it was-"*first day, second, third, fourth, fifth sixth and Saturday or Shabbat*".

The Gregorian Calendar[25]

The Gregorian Calendar is a revision of the Julian Calendar or a more up-to-date version. It was implemented based on the declarations of the Council of Nicaea and is called Gregorian from the year 1582 and by the name of Pope Gregory XIII.

The Gregorian reform was born from the need to put into practice one of the agreements of the Council of Trent: to adjust the calendar to eliminate the gap produced since the first Council of Nicaea that was celebrated in 325. The astral moment at which Easter (Saturnalia, Sun Invictus, Tammuz...) was to be celebrated and, in connection with it, the other movable religious holidays had been fixed.

In short, what mattered was the regularity of the liturgical calendar, for which it was necessary to introduce certain corrections in the civil calendar. Basically, it was about adapting the *civil calendar* to the tropical year. This is the calendar that was accepted worldwide and used in most of the world.

So far we have seen different types of calendars and how they are all governed until we reach the Gregorian calendar, the one used in most countries. We must remember that the Gregorian calendar is the calendar created by Pope Gregory XIII, in other words, it is the Roman and Catholic calendar or coming from the reform of Constantine; the sun and the moon are observed to create the times and epochs.

25

However, in the Middle Ages and after the fall of Rome, Christianity firmly prevailed. January 1st was considered too pagan date, that's why many countries where Christianity dominated wanted the new year to be marked on March 25th.

Finally, Pope Gregory XIII introduced the Gregorian calendar and January 1st was reinstated as the New Year in Catholic countries. In England, however, who had rebelled against the authority of the Pope and professed the Protestant religion, it continued to be celebrated on March 25 until the year 1752.

Biblical Calendar

Finally we can share some points about the biblical calendar which is found and governed under the scriptural norms given by **YAHUAH** to his people. Many around the world use this calendar because it is the one established in the Bible and not one that follows the dispositions of men or institutions that only seek their own benefit.

To conclude, we talked earlier about the different types of existing calendars and how through the ages people have been governed by the moon, the sun, the constellations, the seasons and nature in general to define the times and epochs, and the days. In the end, everything is based on what people understand as the beginning of the day.

2024

Notes:

March 20: First day of the biblical year.

April 2 – 9: Passover (*sundown to sundown* – Unleavened Bread (Lev 23: 4-8, Num 33:3, Ex 12). *Sundown to sundown.*

* **April 26:** First Fruits. Day of offering. (Lev. 23:1-2, 9-14) *Sunrise to sunrise.*

Mayo 26: Pentecost (Lev 23:9-16, Ex 34:22, 23:16, Num 28:26, Deut.16:10, Jub. 1:1, 6:15-22, 44:1-5) *Sunrise to sunrise.*

September 16: Trumpets (Lev 23:23-25, Num 29:1-6) *Sunrise to sunrise.*

September 25: Atonement (Lev 23:27, 32, 16:29-31) *Fasting – Sundown to sundown.*

October 1-8: Tabernacles (Lev 23:33-36, Job 16:20-31, 32:16) *Sunrise to sunrise.*

* Days with underscore: First day of each month. Blessing at the beginning of the month. *Starting on March 20, 2024*

* **Shabbath (Saturdays)** days to rest. *70 biblical holidays in a year.*

* **Tithing:** (Deut 14:23-28, 26:16) every three years. Next tithing on march 2026. www.yahuahbible.com

January

S	M	T	W	T	F	S
	1	2	3	4	5	6
7	8	9	10	11	12	13
14	15	16	17	18	19	20
21	22	23	24	25	26	27
28	29	30	31			

February

S	M	T	W	T	F	S
				1	2	3
4	5	6	7	8	9	10
11	12	13	14	15	16	17
18	19	20	21	22	23	24
25	26	27	28	29		

March

S	M	T	W	T	F	S
					1	2
3	4	5	6	7	8	9
10	11	12	13	14	15	16
17	18	19	20	21	22	23
24	25	26	27	28	29	30
31						

April

S	M	T	W	T	F	S
	1	2	3	4	5	6
7	8	9	10	11	12	13
14	15	16	17	18	19	20
21	22	23	24	25	26	27
28	29	30				

May

S	M	T	W	T	F	S
			1	2	3	4
5	6	7	8	9	10	11
12	13	14	15	16	17	18
19	20	21	22	23	24	25
26	27	28	29	30	31	

June

S	M	T	W	T	F	S
						1
2	3	4	5	6	7	8
9	10	11	12	13	14	15
16	17	18	19	20	21	22
23	24	25	26	27	28	29
30						

July

S	M	T	W	T	F	S
	1	2	3	4	5	6
7	8	9	10	11	12	13
14	15	16	17	18	19	20
21	22	23	24	25	26	27
28	29	30	31			

August

S	M	T	W	T	F	S
				1	2	3
4	5	6	7	8	9	10
11	12	13	14	15	16	17
18	19	20	21	22	23	24
25	26	27	28	29	30	31

September

S	M	T	W	T	F	S
1	2	3	4	5	6	7
8	9	10	11	12	13	14
15	16	17	18	19	20	21
22	23	24	25	26	27	28
29	30					

October

S	M	T	W	T	F	S
		1	2	3	4	5
6	7	8	9	10	11	12
13	14	15	16	17	18	19
20	21	22	23	24	25	26
27	28	29	30	31		

November

S	M	T	W	T	F	S
					1	2
3	4	5	6	7	8	9
10	11	12	13	14	15	16
17	18	19	20	21	22	23
24	25	26	27	28	29	30

December

S	M	T	W	T	F	S
1	2	3	4	5	6	7
8	9	10	11	12	13	14
15	16	17	18	19	20	21
22	23	24	25	26	27	28
29	30	31				

Start of the Day

First of all, many people say that the day starts from midnight, that's why today 12:01 is already part of the next day. However, that theory is wrong and false.

Others say that the day starts in the afternoon, after 6pm, and that's why they start counting the day from this moment until 6pm the next day. This is also a wrong theory.

On the other hand, there are those who say that the beginning of the day is with the first sunlight and they start the day from the first rays of the sun until the second before the first rays of the sun of the next morning or the next day. This theory is also wrong, however, it is the closest to the truth.

All these errors and misinterpretations are a consequence of the different translations of the Bible into other languages. We do not understand the Hebrew term used and then we come to wrong conclusions about the topic or about the beginning of the day. However, the answer is simpler than we think and has always been there. In fact, our ancestors, who could neither read nor write, did know the answer to what humanity is confused about today.

I remember perfectly that my grandmother and grandfather got up very early in the morning to work and the idea was before "dawn breaks". It's amazing, they didn't know about letters or studies, but they weren't confused in their thoughts. They knew that the day began with the "Dawn", not with the moon nor the sun. They knew that before the sun rose there was a clarity called "Dawn" and this was the one that marked the beginning of the day. "From Latin *albus*, the **alba**[26] it refers to the **sunrise** or to the **first appearance light of the day** in the sky before the **Sunshine**."

Before Dawn there is a moment of darkness, which represents the end of the previous day; there then appears the Dawn that marks the beginning of the new day and then the sun appears. That's how nature works. It is enough to observe and realize to understand what the beginning of a new day indicates to us. We call this the Biblical day according to the creation of **YAHUAH ELOHIYM**.

Berēshith 1:3-5 *3 And **ĔLÔHÎYM** said, Let there be light: and there was light. 4 And **ĔLÔHÎYM** saw the light, that it was good: and **ĔLÔHÎYM** divided the light from the darkness. 5 And **ĔLÔHÎYM** called the light Day, and the darkness he called Night. And the evening and the morning were the first day.*

Be light and was light: the term used in Hebrew for the word light is Ôr (אוֹר), and it means "illumination, including the rays, happiness, clarity, day, light, morning and sun". This tells us that the lights were created at that moment and that that light marks the beginning of the new day, not necessarily the sun.

Berēshith 32: *24 And Yaăqôb was left alone; and there wrestled a man with him until the breaking of the **day**.*

Berēshith 32: *26 And he said, Let me go, for the **day breaks**. And he said, I will not let you go, except you bless me.*

26

In verses 24 and 26 he tells us "until the breaking of the day", however, in Hebrew , it uses the term Elâh (עָלָה) which means *to ascend, to rise up* and the second term used for the word day is Shachar (שַׁחַר) which means *dawn or dawn: - early day, morning light.* Where does it come from?

What we are literally seeing in these verses is the beginning of the day or the first light of day, or the beginning of the day, which is synonymous with the breaking of day. Then it is perfectly understandable and visible that the day begins at dawn or at first light in the morning.

Remember that in **Berēshiṯh 1** everything on the first day of creation began with the light. Do not forget that there was no sunrise until the fourth day of creation.

This is why many of us observe and start our days at the break of dawn, with the first light of dawn, that is, according to the Bible.

This makes the biblical calendar fall on different dates than the Gregorian calendar, since all the months in the Bible have 30 days (12 x 30 = 360). Most of the 7 most important Biblical holidays fall on different dates on the Gregorian calendar. For example, the first month of the year according to the Bible and according to the words of **YAHUAH** it is March - April of the Gregorian calendar. That is, the month of Âbîyb. **Shemōṯh 12:2** *This month will be the beginning of the months for you; this will be the first one for you in the months of the year.*

In the **Book of Jubilees** we read the following verses in order to understand how the world is.

Jubilees 6: *36 For there will surely be those who will make observations of the moon, how (she) disturbs the seasons and arrives from year to year* **ten days earlier**. *37 therefore there will come upon them years when they will disturb (the order), and they will make (day)* **abominable on the day of testimony**, *and* **dirty day of the holiday, and they shall confound the holy one with the unclean one every day, and the unclean day with the holy one; for they shall err concerning the months and Shabbath and feasts and Jubilees.** *38 therefore I command you, and bear witness unto you, that you may bear witness unto them; for after your death your sons (shall) trouble them, so that they shall not make the year three hundred and sixty-four days only (364), and* **for this reason they will be mistaken about the new months and seasons and Shabbath and festivals, and they will eat all kinds of blood with all kinds of flesh.**

In these verses we can see some important points that we should pay attention to.

Observations of the Moon: those who rule cults and give worship to the moon as a deity.

Dirty day of the holiday: those who have corrupted the feasts of **YAHUAH** for pagan holidays and they have changed the date (days and months) making then that the world celebrates its pagan holidays.

They will confuse the days, the holy one with the unclean one... they will be mistaken about the months, Saturdays, feasts and jubilation: the same thing we are seeing today, people no longer make a distinction between the holy day and the unclean day. All days are the same for the world, Saturday is no longer the Shabbath for them because they have changed it; also, they have even abolished holidays and there are no jubilees anymore.

These verses tell about our time and how the world is today. Let's reflect, think, scrutinize, retain the good and act before it's too late.

CHAPTER IX

---◈◆◈---

EXECUTIONERS AND
PERSECUTORS OF THE FOLLOWERS
OF YAHUAH

S ometimes it is very easy to forget about the vicissitudes and storms that our ancestors went through so that today we have all the freedoms we have; I could make a recount from the Old Testament. However, for a more adequate understanding, we will start with the New Testament.

First of all, do we forget the executioners and executors of **YAHUSHA?** They are, in fact, the same ones who persecuted the followers of **YAHUSHA,** or rather to his disciples. Let us remember Saul of Tarsus, better known today as the Apostle Paul.

What was Saul's primary occupation? Persecute the followers of **YAHUSHA**, since he was a Pharisee. They have been the main persecutors, executioners and public enemies of **YAHUAH, YAHUSHA** and everything that had to do with our Creator and Savior.

Then they continued to persecute the apostles, the early church and all the followers of **YAHUSHA**; to all those who kept the Shabbath and the Biblical feasts.

Revelation 3: [9] *"Behold, I am delivering up from the synagogue of Satan those who **they say they are Yahudiy and they are not** but they are lying; behold, I will cause them to come and bow down at your feet, and to acknowledge that I have loved you."* They claim to be **YAHUAH**'s people, but in reality they are not. They were supplanted and planted in Yâshârêl from other nations. When Yâshârêl was conquered, its inhabitants were scattered all over the world and brought new inhabitants from many nations to populate the nation of Yâshârêl.

This is the same group that was present with Constantine, the one who has persecuted, executed and imprisoned throughout history all those who oppose his new god and new religion, breaking, consequently, the commandments of **YAHUAH**, His Shabbath day (Saturday) and His feasts.

YAHUSHA he tells us a lot of things about the Pharisees, and believe me, they are not good. We sometimes read the Bible, but we don't stop to think or meditate on what we read. So let's look at some key verses.

Matthew 23: *[3]So, whatever they tell you to keep, keep it and do it; **but do not do according to their works, for they say, and do not**.*

Matthew 23: *[1] But woe to you, scribes and Pharisees, hypocrites! for you shut up the kingdom of heaven from men; for neither do you enter, **nor do you let***

in those who are entering.

Mark 7: *⁵So the Pharisees and the scribes asked him, "Why don't your disciples walk according to **the tradition of the elders** but do they eat bread with unclean hands? ⁶He answered and said to them, "Hypocrites, Yeshayâhû prophesied well about you, as it is written, 'This people honors me with their lips, but their heart is far from me.'*

According to **YAHUSHA,** we should not do what the Pharisees do, since they are an impediment to entering the kingdom of **YAHUAH.** So much so that with their traditions they block the entrance to the kingdom of **YAHUAH.** Let's look at some of the main characteristics of the scribes and Pharisees according to **Matthew 23**.

● **Hypocrites:** with their traditions, doctrines and rituals contradict the law of **YAHUAH.** Everything they do is a show for others to see, and so they are deceiving and driving people away from **YAHUAH.** *¹⁴ Woe to you, scribes and Pharisees, **hypocrites**! because you devour widows' houses, and make long prayers as a pretext; for this you will receive greater condemnation.*

● **They close the kingdom of heaven:** They keep people out of the kingdom; they are stumbling blocks and drive people out of the synagogues. *¹³But woe to you, scribes and Pharisees, hypocrites! Because **you shut up the kingdom of heaven before men** for you do not enter yourselves, nor do you allow those who are entering to enter.*

● **Misrepresenting The Scriptures**: they twist the scriptures according to their own convenience and thus create so-called gaps in order to break the commandments. *¹⁶ Woe to you, blind guides! that you say, If anyone swears by the temple, it is nothing; but if anyone swears by the gold of the temple, he is a debtor.*

● **Guides for the blind:** They do not practice justice nor are they merciful. *⁷⁷ Woe to you, scribes and Pharisees, hypocrites! because you tithe the mint and the dill and the cumin, and **you leave out the most important of the law: justice, mercy and faith**. This needed to be done, while still doing that. ²⁴ Blind guides, you strain the mosquito, and swallow the camel!*

● **Self-righteous and self-indulgent:** Being self-righteous and believing themselves to be the best, they look for faults in others. *²⁵ Woe to you, scribes and Pharisees, hypocrites! because you clean the outside of the glass and the plate, **but inside you are full of theft and injustice**. ²⁶ You blind Pharisee! Clean the inside of the glass and the plate first, so that the outside is also clean.*

● **The dead and the spiritually unclean:** They are spiritually dead, therefore they can only lead to the spiritual death of those who follow them. *²⁷ Woe to you, scribes and Pharisees, hypocrites! because you are similar to **white sepulchers**, which on the outside, to the truth, show themselves beautiful, **but inside they are full of the bones of the dead and all filth**.*

● **They will not escape the fire of hell:** they are snakes and generation of vipers so they will have no escape. Also, since they know that their days are numbered, they want to drag the whole of humanity with them *33 Snakes, generation of vipers! ¿How will* **you escape the condemnation of hell**?

● **Murderers:** they lamented that their ancestors were the authors of the death of the prophets; however, they were themselves the instigators and executioners. This is how they led our Savior to death **YAHUSHA**, persecuted the disciples and apostles, and continue and will continue to persecute the followers of **YAHUSHA**. *34Therefore, behold, I am sending you prophets and wise men and scribes; and of them, to some* **you will kill and impale**, *and to others* **you will flog** *in your synagogues, and* **will persecute** *from city to city.*

Perhaps many people think that the Pharisees and scribes eventually ceased to exist, but unfortunately this is not the case. They simply changed their organization or name and assumed even more power in the world. As a result, they created chaos and corrupted the commandments of **YAHUAH**. We only have to read the ecclesiastical history or general history to realize the reality.

When the Pharisees and scribes in our century saw that they could no longer contain or follow up the massacres of the past, they hid behind the Roman Empire and decided to comply to the letter with this verse, **Matthew 7**: [15]*Beware of false prophets, who come to you in sheep's clothing, but inside they are ravenous wolves.*

They then disguised themselves as followers (sheep) of **YAHUAH** in order to corrode, corrupt and contaminate the true sheep from the inside, since they do not realize that they are rapacious wolves whose sole objective is to distance humanity from **YAHUAH** and lead them down the wide road that only leads to perdition. They, dressed as sheep although wolves inside, will continue to persecute and confuse humanity until the end of time. **Matthew 24**: *²²And if those days were not shortened, **no one would be saved**; but for the sake of the elect, those days will be shortened*. The deception and deception are so great that even the chosen ones would be deceived. **Matthew 24**: *²⁴For false messiahs and false prophets will arise and will perform great signs and wonders, so that they will deceive, if possible, even the elect.*

However, these rapacious wolves and humanity in general are forgetting something very important, **2 Peter 3**: *⁸But, O beloved, do not be ignorant of this: that for **YAHUSHA (YAHUAH)** a day is like a thousand years, and a thousand years like a day.*

The golden rule that we have all ignored and forgotten is that for **YAHUAH** one day is like a thousand years and a thousand years are like one day. The deceptions, disappointments and tricks are coming to an end as well as the time that humanity has left. Sin will have its just retribution and this time it will be permanent. **Berēshīth 2**: *¹⁷ But of the tree of the knowledge of good and evil, you shall not eat of it: for in the day that you eat thereof you shall surely die.*

This was the warning given to Âdâm, and mankind has forgotten that **YAHUAH** he said that the very same day the man sinned or ate from the tree, he die. It is important to emphasize that he was not talking about a spiritual death as some say, but he was referring to physical death. This is the reason why there is no human being who has reached the age of a thousand (one day to **YAHUAH**), because the very same day we are born, we die and it is thanks to original sin.

This indicates to us that **YAHUAH** is not relaxed and that this is not a game. Some people say, but why **YAHUAH** does it allow so many things? What we don't understand is that for **YAHUAH** humanity has not yet turned 7 days (7,000 years).

In the same way that **YAHUAH** in 7 days he created everything that exists (with the exception of demons, which were the creation of man and angels), seven days he is giving his creation to return to its origin. The problem is that we are so peculiar that instead of turning in pursuit of **YAHUAH**, we turn in pursuit of evil and thus force **YAHUAH** to SAVE the few ones from his creation once again by destroying all evil, but this time with fire, as he did with Sedôm and Ămôrâh.

Do not forget that we are almost entering the end of the sixth day of creation (approximately 6,895 thousand years). This means that, although many people think it's late, the end is coming and it's closer than we think. The seventh day or day of rest (Shabbath) is the day of rest for **YAHUAH**, is when **YAHUSHA** will be enjoying his reign for a day (a thousand years). Then, the end will come.

Idols

This is the definition of the word Idol according to

the RAE: *"Image of a deity object of worship. Person or thing loved or admired with exaltation."*

This indicates to us that any deity or supposed ELOHIYM who is the object of worship or reverence is an idol, including any person or thing that we have as exalted in such a way that we worship or reverence him, making him take the place of **YAHUAH** in our lives.

It is so much so that the term idol has taken a new turn in all of humanity to such a level that it is not strange to hear saying *"that's my idol"*, referring to a public figure, artist and other celebrities. An idol is also known in the Bible as "false god or false gods".

In other words, the most hated term in the Bible has become something common and normal in our society. We conclude then that an idol is when something or someone becomes more important to us than **YAHUAH**.

Wayyīqrā 26: [1] *You shall make you no idols nor graven image, neither rear you up a standing image, neither shall you set up any image of stone in your land, to bow down unto it: for I am* **YAHUAH** *your* **ĔLÔHÎYM** .

The word used for idol is Ĕlîyl (אֱלִיל) and means *"good for nothing, vain or vanity; idol, worthless, thing of nothing."* This is an idol according to the Bible and according to the Hebrew text; in other words, people change **YAHUAH** for nothing, something good for nothing and worthless.

Idolatry

Idolatry is worshipping an idol or image of a deity or offering worship to it. Such a deity or idol takes the place of **YAHUAH** and it is worshipped as if it were, that is, it is the veneration, love or worship of an idol.

It we read our Bible carefully, there is not a single good or positive reference about idolatry. In fact, this practice is roundly condemned throughout the Bible. So much so that the first commandment is against this abominable practice.

Šhemōṭh 20: [3-5] *You shall have no other gods before me. You shall not make unto you any graven image, or any likeness of anything that is in heaven above, or that is in the earth beneath, or that is in the water under the earth. You shall not bow down yourself to them, nor serve them: for I **YAHUAH** your **ĔLÔHÎYM** am a jealous **ÊL,** visiting the iniquity of the fathers upon the children unto the third and fourth generation of them that hate me.*

If we say that we believe in the Bible and read it frequently, we also claim to know the commandments, which are the same all over the world, with the exception of some religious entity that has shortened it or removed some parts. However, in the end they are the same commandments for all mankind.

How is it that we are still in this abhorrent practice of idolatry? Idols and idolatry have been the main problem of the people of **YAHUAH** since the fall, man has been prostituting himself to other false gods, worshipping them, and forgetting the laws, precepts, and statutes of **YAHUAH**.

Sometimes we want to present ourselves as self-righteous and condemn the people of Yâshârêl for their constant prostitution with pagan gods and forgetfulness of their Creator **YAHUAH**; however, what difference is there today?

We are in the same, or worse and when we have the rope around our neck because we can no longer stand the problems or oppression, then we cry out to **YAHUAH** to set us free. And thanks to his infinite kindness, **YAHUAH** sets us free. And as time passes, we are blessed and prospered, and we again forget about **YAHUAH** and prostitute ourselves to pagan gods, and the cycle repeats itself every day of our lives. Let's reflect and rethink before it's too late.

False or pagan gods in the Bible

This is a list of the main false or pagan gods found in the Bible. You can visit the Bible verses for more information or search the internet to know any details about these pagan deities.

2 Melāķîm 7: 31	2 Melāķîm17: 30	2 Melāķîm 1: 1-6	2 Melāķîm 19: 37	2 Melāķîm 5: 18	1 Melāķîm 11: 5
Nibhaz	Sukkot-benot	Baal-zebub (Beelzebub)	Nisroc	Rimmon	Astoret
Tartac	Nergal				Milcom
Adramelech	Asima				
Anamelec					
Šemôţh 34: 13	**Yirmeyâhû 7: 9**	**Šôphţîm 16: 23**	**Yeshayâhû 46: 2**	**Yechezqêl 8: 14**	**Acts 14: 12 & 19: 24**
Asherah-	*Baal (there are many combinations with the name of this deity)	Dagon	Bel	Tammuz	Jupiter
			Nebo		Mercury
					Diana (Artemisa)

143

CHAPTER X

SALVATION

S ome people get confused and ask how people could be saved in the Old Testament; but salvation has never changed, it has always been the same.

Ephesians 2: *⁸ For it is by grace you have been saved through faith, and that not of yourselves, it is the gift of **ELOHIYM**. ⁹ not by works, so that no one may boast.*

Chăbaqqûq 2: *⁴ Behold, he whose soul is not upright is proud; but the righteous shall live by his faith.*

Grace through faith is the key to salvation. If we understand that by grace we are safe and this is a free and undeserved gift that comes directly from **YAHUAH**, then we are saved. The saving sacrifice made for the forgiveness of our sins with the death of our Savior **YAHUSHA**, gives us access to the throne of grace and salvation or eternal life.

John 14: [6] *YAHUSHA said to him, I am the way, and the truth, and the life; no one comes to the Father (**YAHUAH**), but for me (**YAHUSHA**).*

YAHUSHA it is the only way or way to reach the throne of grace and be accepted by our Creator **YAHUAH**, and thus obtaining salvation for our souls. When we accept a **YAHUSHA** as our Savior, from that very moment the blood of **YAHUSHA** poured out on the Calvary rescues and saves us. Then, **YAHUAH** when he looks at us, he sees the blood spilled by **YAHUSHA** and the grace that was given to us in His sacrifice; instead of looking at our faults and uncleanness.

How can you be saved? The answer is clear in these Bible verses. **Acts 16:** [30] *and he brought them out, and said to them, Gentlemen, what must I do to be saved?* [31] *They said, Believe in the Master **YAHUSHA** the Mâshîyach, and you will be saved, you and your house.* Once again, you just have to believe in **YAHUSHA** the Mâshîyach, confessing him with your mouth and believing with your heart. This is salvation.

Let us not forget that salvation has a future connotation and this is the certainty that we all seek. We all want to know, where will we spend eternity? When we talk about salvation, we are mostly referring to the future or eternal state of our souls.

This is the question that haunts our minds, will it be for eternal damnation or eternal salvation? Or where will it be? We must remember some important points in order to better understand the final destination of each person.

When a person dies, according to **YAHUSHA, that** person enters into a dream state **John 11**: [11] *having said this, he said to them afterwards: Our friend Lazarus **sleep** but I'm going to wake him up.*

We are just like the disciples who did not understand when YAHUSHA told them that Lazarus was sleeping; but **YAHUSHA** told them that he was dead, because when we die we enter a stage of sleep.

Nowhere in the Bible is it written that when we die we go to heaven; this is not a biblical belief. So much so that the Bible does not say that we are going to heaven in any state or moment of our existence. Heaven was not created for humans, the earth is the place that **YAHUAH** created for us. It is so much so that **YAHUSHA** brings the new Yerûshâlaim to earth to dwell with us.

When we die, we enter the tomb or sepulchral chamber (dream state) where we await the resurrection. **John 5**: [28] *Marvel not at this: for the hour is coming, in the which all that are in the graves shall hear his voice, [29] And shall come forth; they that have done good, unto the resurrection of life; and they that have done evil, unto the resurrection of damnation.*

We all hear His voice, but some will be resurrected for eternal damnation and others for eternal salvation.

Those of us who are raised to eternal life will spend our eternity in the new Yerûshâlaim (not in heaven), rather in the tabernacle of **YAHUAH** which is the New Yerûshâlaim coming down from heaven. Those who are resurrected for condemnation, those who do not find their names in the book of life, then they will be consumed by eternal fire. **Matthew 25:** [46] *And these will go away to eternal punishment, and the righteous to eternal life.*

Let's recapitulate:

● Salvation is only through the blood shed on the Calvary for the forgiveness of our sins. That is, only **YAHUSHA** gives us salvation, no one and nothing else.

● When we die, we enter a dream state. You're not going to heaven and you're not going to hell. You go directly to the chamber of the tomb where you will wait to be judged on the Day of Judgment. **Qōheleṯh 9:** [5-6] *For those who live know that they must die, but the dead know nothing, and have no more wages, for their memory is forgotten. [6]Their love and their hatred and their envy have also passed away, and they will no longer have a part in everything that is done under the sun.* And since we are sleeping, there is nothing more that can be done, you only have the opportunity while you are alive. The dead neither feel nor suffer. Only while you are alive you can do it, choose who you want to serve. Choose the wide path or the narrow one.

At the Second Coming of **YAHUSHA** those of us who have died following Him as our Savior will be resurrected, and those of us who are alive at that moment and who are serving Him from the heart will be lifted up on the clouds to join our Savior. **1 Thessalonians 4:** [16-17] [16]*For the **YAHUSHA** himself shall descend from heaven with a shout, with the voice of the archangel, and with the trump of **ELOHIYM**: and the dead in Messiah shall rise* first: *17 Then we which are alive and remain shall be caught up together with them in the clouds, to meet* **YAHUSHA** *in the air: and so shall we ever be with* **YAHUSHA**. This is where most people get confused, because will meet him in the air... of course, he is coming down, so we will meet him in the air before establishing on earth, but we are not going up, we are coming down with him.

● We reign with **YAHUSHA** on this earth for a thousand years. **Revelation 20**: *4 And I saw thrones, and those who received the faculty of judging sat on them; and I saw the souls of those who were beheaded because of the testimony of* **YAHUSHA** *and because of the word of* **ELOHIYM**, *those who had not worshipped the beast or his image, and who did not receive the mark on their foreheads or on their hands;* **and they lived and reigned with the Mâshîyach a thousand years**.

● After this, those who died since the beginning of mankind and those who died without **YAHUSHA** in their lives, they will be resurrected for the **day of the Last Judgment** they will receive a just reward for their deeds. That is, they will receive salvation or eternal damnation. **Revelation 20**: *5-6 But the other dead did not live again until a thousand years were completed. This is the first resurrection. 6Blessed and holy is he who has a part in the first resurrection; the second death has no power over these, but they will be Kohen of* **ELOHIYM** *and of the Mâshîyach, and will reign with him a thousand years.* It is here that the wicked will be thrown into eternal fire, **Revelation 20**: *14 And death and Hades were cast into the lake of fire. This is the second death. 15 And whoever was not found written in the book of life* *was thrown into the lake of fire.*

● BUT there is a great news for all of us who are part of the chosen ones, the ones receiving eternal life, we will all receive NEW BODIES, just like **YAHUSHA** when he came back from death. ONLY the righteous will receive new bodies, the wicked will be consumed. **Philippians 3**:21 *who shall change our vile body (corrupt bodies, our current bodies), that it may be fashioned like unto his glorious body (our new bodies), according to the working whereby he is able even to subdue all things unto himself.*

● Because we will need our new bodies to enter the New Yerûshâlaim. The New Yerûshâlaim clearly described in **Revelation 21**: ² *And I John saw the holy city, the new Yerûshâlaim, coming down from heaven, from* ***ELOHIYM****, prepared as a bride adorned for her husband.*

That is, it comes down from heaven to be established on earth where we will dwell with our Creator **YAHUAH**. Nowhere in scripture does it say that we humans are going to heaven. This does not happen, it is not biblical. The earth is our paradise that was created for us and we corrupt it with sin, that's why we need our new home that will replace this corrupt earth with the spotless New Yerûshâlaim. But everything will happen here, we are earthly beings and on earth we will always be, heaven is not for us humans so we will never go to heaven.

I hope we can understand the gravity and brevity of the current situation in which we find ourselves. For those who want to have safe passage or free passage to eternal life, only **YAHUSHA** can give it and there is only possibility while we are alive.

This is the reason why **YAHUSHA** it is our salvation and only in **YAHUSHA** there is salvation for our souls. There are no more opportunities, **it's HERE AND NOW.** Be very careful what you choose, because your decision is a matter of eternal life or death. **Matthew 24**: [13] *But he who endures to the end, he will be saved*.

Too many people are confused about salvation and they are looking around and trying to learn from other with the fear and doubt whether they are safe or not. Allow me to illustrate this for a better understanding.

There is a street in your city, neighborhood or town and that street is the only one with electric poles. There is no light anywhere else, ONLY that street has electric poles and electricity. Therefore, whoever walks, drives or pass by that street will enjoy the benefit of the light. BUT, if you step outside or drive outside that street; will you find light? Of course not, that street is the ONLY one and the ONLY place with electricity.

You can pretend to walk close to that street, but you will only see the light on others, but the light will not reach you. AND, as long as you are in that street, you will always be in that light. If you step out, you will find yourself walking in darkness, because you left the ONLY street where there is light.

That street is called **YAHUSHA** (*he is the way*), that light in the street is **YAHUSH** (*he is the life*). If you step outside of him, forsake him or leave him, you are automatically out of his way; therefore you no longer enjoy the privileges of him. You need to abide in him to enjoy the things he has already prepared for us. Outside of him, there is NOTHING.

The only thing you have to do is to keep his commandments and nothing else. **John 8**: *51 Verily, verily, I say unto you, if a man keep my saying (word, commandment), he shall never see death.* **John 14**:15 *If you love me, keep my commandments.*

How to develop a relationship with YAHUAH (YAHUSHA)?

We all want to know how to develop a personal relationship with our Creator **YAHUAH** or our Savior **YAHUSHA**.

The truth is that as human beings we always look for the most difficult ways to feel good and say that we are doing something to contribute to our relationship with **YAHUAH.** However, it is simpler than we have been taught and think. These are the three important steps to achieve this relationship:

● **Study the Word of YAHUAH**: by studying His word we can come to know His commandments and statutes for our lives. I always talk about his commandments (10 commandments) and his statutes (keeping his feasts). **John 5**: ³⁹*Search the Scriptures, for it seems to you that in them you have eternal life, and they are the ones who testify about me.* (**YAHUSHA***).*

● Talk to **YAHUAH**: we must remember that a

relationship takes time and that the way to relate is by communicating, talking and sharing with **YAHUAH**. **Tehillim 119**: *[15] I will meditate in your precepts, and have respect unto your ways. [16] I will delight myself in your statutes: I will not forget your word.* **Yahusha 1**: *[8] This book of the law shall not depart out of your mouth; but you shall meditate therein day and night, that you may observe to do according to all that is written therein: for then you shall make your way prosperous, and then you shall have good success.* As we meditate and think about His commandments and statutes, we are sharing with **YAHUAH**, we are delighting in His ordinances and at the same time we are sharing with **YAHUAH** in a natural way instead of turning it into a monotonous ritual. This is our way of communication to constantly talk to our Creator **YAHUAH**. **1 Thessalonians 5**: *[17]Pray without ceasing.* It is not that we are always on our knees, but we are constantly meditating on His word and commandments. In this way we are praying without ceasing and in constant communication with **YAHUAH**.

● **Follow YAHUSHA**: **John 14**: *[6] YAHUSHA said to him, I am the way, and the truth, and the life; no one comes to the Father (**YAHUAH**), but for me (**YAHUSHA**). [7]If you knew me (**YAHUSHA**), also to my Father (**YAHUAH**) would have known; and from now on you know him, and have seen him.* How do we follow **YAHUSHA**? **John 14**: *[15] If you love me, keep my commandments.* That's all we have to do to follow **YAHUSHA**. We must express Him with love after accepting him into our lives, and the only way we show that love is when we keep His commandments. We have already seen that the commandments to

153

which **YAHUSHA** refers to the 10 commandments.

As you can see, these three simple steps are all we need to develop our personal relationship with our Creator **YAHUAH** and our Savior **YAHUSHA**. I don't know if you have noticed, but at no time have I talked about feelings or emotional states. Our relationship and communication with our Creator **YAHUAH** has nothing to do with feelings or how we are.

I've heard so many people say, "It just doesn't work out for me. I just don't feel it. I just don't feel like I'm doing it right." Feelings are treacherous because they are futile and fleeting. Our relationship is based on conviction and action. **Hebrews 11**: [1] *So faith is the certainty of what is hoped for, the conviction of what is not seen.* This is precisely what we need to understand: we are approaching **YAHUSHA** through faith, and faith is action, it is conviction, it is not feelings or words. It is conviction and certainty, or security, in what we do and in what we believe.

The Chosen Ones

In most cases, we do not pay attention or rather we do not stop to think about this topic and, then, the reality of it escapes from our perspective and from our life. We forget that there are the chosen, the privileged, the favorites or the seed of **YAHUAH**; whatever qualification you want to use is fine with me.

YAHUAH created everything and on the sixth day he decides to create man (corporal) in his image or likeness; it is his most perfect work and for which he has created everything. **YAHUAH** is pleased with his creation and gives it to Âdâm and Chawwâh to take care of and enjoy.

Berëshîṯh 2: [15] *And* **YAHUAH ĔLÔHÎYM** *took Âdâm, and put him into the Garden of Eden to dress it and to keep it.* However, Âdâm and Chawwâh disobeyed and brought sin, or disobedience, for the first time since creation and as a result are expelled from the Garden of Eden, or better known as paradise. **YAHUAH** expels them because nothing corrupt or impure can enjoy the paradise created by him.

Berëshîṯh 3: [23] *Therefore* **YAHUAH ĔLÔHÎYM** *sent him forth from the Garden of Eden, to till the ground from whence he was taken.* [24] *So he drove out the man; and he placed at the east of the garden of Eden Kerûb, and a flaming sword which turned every way, to keep the way of the tree of life.*

Then humanity begins to be populated and we find that disobedience and pollution are so great in creation that **YAHUAH** decides to safeguard the only pure thing that remains of it. Save the chosen ones: Nôach and his relatives (eight in total).

Berëshîṯh 6: [18-20] *But with you I will establish my covenant; and you shall come into the ark, you, and your sons, and your wife, and your sons' wives with you.* [19] *And of every living thing of all flesh, two of every sort shall you bring into the ark, to keep them alive with you; they shall be male and female.* [20] *Of fowls after their kind, and of cattle after their kind, of every creeping thing of the earth after his kind, two of every sort shall come unto you, to keep them alive.*

Then, the history of mankind continues, however,

the corruption and pollution of **YAHUAH**'s creation is again so horrifying that the time comes to destroy Sedôm and Ămôrâh. But, not before **YAHUAH** saves the elect.

Berēshīṯh 19: ¹⁹⁻²⁰ *Behold now, your servant has found grace in your sight, and you have magnified your mercy, which you have showed unto me in saving my life; and I cannot escape to the mountain, lest some evil take me, and I die:* ²⁰ *Behold now, this city is near to flee unto, and it is a little one: Oh, let me escape thither, (is it not a little one?) and my soul shall live.*

Since humanity had advanced so much, **YAHUAH** then decides that it is time to hand over His Law to His chosen people. And that is why on Mount Sîynay **YAHUAH** passes his 10 commandments for his chosen people to Môsheh.

This law was not given to all the neighboring nations, much less to the whole world, but it was given to the chosen people of Yâshârêl. But the funny thing is that when **YAHUAH** gives the commandments to Môsheh, he also includes the Gentile (not a Yâshârêl) and the foreigner who lived in the land of Yâshârêl and wanted to be part of the people.

Shemōṯh 19: ⁵⁻⁶ *Now therefore, if you will obey my voice indeed, and keep my covenant, then you shall be a peculiar treasure unto me above all people: for all the earth is mine:* ⁶ *And you shall be unto me a kingdom of* **kôhên**, *and a holy nation. These are the words which you shall speak unto the children of Yâshârêl.*

In other words, **YAHUAH** grants citizenship to anyone who would like to be part of His people, regardless of whether they were a foreigner or a pagan. If he wanted to be part of and follow the law of **YAHUAH**, then he was naturalized; he became a citizen of Yâshârêl and became part of the chosen people.

Wayyīqrā 19: [33] *And if a stranger sojourn with you in your land, you shall not vex him.* [34] *But the stranger that dwells with you shall be unto you as one born among you, and you shall love him as yourself; for you were strangers in the land of Mitsrayim: I am* **YAHUAH** *your* **ĔLÔHÎYM.**

I hope you remember the story of Râchâb, the harlot who lived in the city of Yerîychô when Yahusha (Joshua) conquered that city. Râchâb was not a Yâshârêl nor did she belong to the people of Yâshârêl; she was a Gentile, a pagan, a harlot or a prostitute. However, she protected the spies and consequently was adopted into the people of Yâshârêl as part of it. The most amazing thing about this story is that Râchâb had two sons; one of them was Bôaz, from where King Dâwid came and, consequently, from where the Mâshîyach **YAHUSHA** came. That is to say, that from a foreigner who became a citizen of **YAHUAH**'s people, the Mâshîyach then came as the Savior of His people.

Matthew 1: [5] *Salmon begat from* **Râchâb** *Bôaz, Bôaz begat* Ôbêd *from Ruth, and* Ôbêd *begat Yishay.* [6] *Yishay begat King* Dâwid, *and King* Dâwid *begat Shelômôh by her who was* Ûrîyâhû's *wife.*

It is the same concept as when you immigrate to another country, say, for example, Italy. You will be a foreigner in Italy until you do all the legal process and the Italian government grants you citizenship.

From that moment on, you will already be an Italian citizen, even if you were not born, raised or have the natural blood of Italians in you. He is now a citizen and therefore enjoys all the privileges that native Italians have and, in addition and in the same way, he has the same responsibilities and must comply with the same laws.

Wayyīqrā 24: [22] *You shall have one manner of law, as well for the stranger, as for one of your own country: for I am* **YAHUAH** *your* **ĔLÔHÎYM**.

In conclusion, this is the same concept that **YAHUAH** has always been available so that anyone who wishes to be part of His people can become a citizen of the kingdom. Since we are already citizens of **YAHUAH**'s kingdom, we then have the obligation and privilege to obey **YAHUAH**'s laws because the law was given to **YAHUAH**'s people directly, not to all mankind.

Similarly, **YAHUAH** decides to create His Feasts (7 a year) to reveal Himself to His people through them. These Feasts were given only to the people of **YAHUAH** and not to the whole world, nor to all the nations. They were given only to the elect.

Wayyīqrā 23: [1-2] *And* **YAHUAH** *spoke unto Môsheh, saying,* [2] *Speak unto the children of Yâshârêl, and say unto them, concerning the feasts of* **YAHUAH**, *which you shall proclaim to be holy convocations, even these are my feasts.*

Humanity continues its course and **YAHUAH** is revealing Himself to His people, to the Elect, throughout history. However, **YAHUAH** only reveals himself to the chosen and not to the whole world. It is so much so, that **YAHUAH** decides to send His only son **YAHUSHA** to die on the Calvary in order that His people, that is, the elect, may be reconciled with **YAHUAH**.

1 John 4: *¹⁰ Herein is love, not that we loved ELOHIYM, but that he (YAHUAH) loved us, and sent his Son (YAHUSHA) to be the propitiation for our sins.*

YAHUSHA came to give eternal life only to those who receive him and confess his name. **John 1**:*¹² But to all who received him, to those who believe in his name, he gave the right to become children of ELOHIYM.* The concept is only for those who receive it, it is not for everyone or for the whole of humanity; it is solely and exclusively for the chosen ones.

Surprisingly, it does not end there, as **YAHUSHA** then says that He must return for His people, for the Elect. He does not return for the entire humanity, but only and exclusively for His people, for the Elect. The most impressive thing of all is that **YAHUSHA** is preparing a dwelling place for us with **YAHUAH**. Even though we spoil everything, **YAHUAH** continues to create a special place for His chosen ones.

John 14: *² In my Father's house (YAHUAH) are many mansions: if it were not so, I (YAHUSHA) would have told you. I (YAHUSHA) go to prepare a place for you. 3 And if I go and prepare a place for you, I will come again, and receive you unto myself; that where I am, there you may be also.*

Now, as it has been since the beginning of mankind, nothing impure or sinful can enter or enjoy the paradise created for us. **YAHUAH** must once again save the elect and definitively condemn or consume the non-elect, the children of perdition. **YAHUAH** must cleanse or purify his creation so that only the elect or pure come to enjoy the created paradise.

Revelation 21: ²⁷ *He will not enter into it* (New Yerûshâlaim) *nothing unclean, or that does abomination and falsehood, but only those who are inscribed* (**only those who are registered, no one else**) *in the Lamb's book of life* (**YAHUSHA**).

In short, this is the concept that I hope is clear to all of us. The creation was not made for the unclean or the corrupt, but the creation was created for the people of **YAHAUH**. Nothing impure or corrupt will ever be able to prevail or enter the paradise created by **YAHUAH**.

This is why, throughout history, **YAHUAH** has always preserved His people or seed, because everything He made is good so that nothing that is not will be able to enjoy or coexist with the goodness of **YAHUAH**.

John 11: ²⁶ *And everyone who lives and believes in me will not die forever. Do you believe this?*

Acts 10: ⁴³ *To him all the prophets bear witness that through his name everyone who believes in him will receive forgiveness of sins.*

1 John 5: ¹ *Everyone who believes that* **YAHUSHA** *is the Mâshîyach is born of* **ELOHIYM**; *and everyone who loves the one he begot, also loves the one who has been begotten by him.*

In other words, unfortunately for many and no matter how hard or bitter it may be to accept, in the end everything will belong to the group of the elect, to those who believe in **YAHUSHA**, to the people of **YAHUAH**. And since **YAHUSHA** is our ambassador, only **YAHUSHA** can give us the citizenship of **YAHUAH**'s kingdom and, therefore, we can now become citizens of **YAHUAH**'s kingdom or people by grace and faith in **YAHUSHA**, our eternal ambassador.

Also, because we are spiritual citizens of **YAHUAH**'s kingdom here on this earth, our laws are YAHUAH's laws. By obeying the King's laws, we get our badge as citizens of the kingdom; and keeping **YAHUAH**'s commandments and remembering and keeping His feasts are signs that we are citizens of His kingdom.

Bemiḏbar 9: ¹⁴ *And if a stranger shall sojourn among you, and will keep the Pesach unto **YAHUAH**; according to the ordinance of the Pesach, and according to the manner thereof, so shall he do: you shall have one ordinance, both for the stranger, and for him that was born in the land.*

Can you call yourself a citizen of **YAHUAH**'s kingdom if you do not obey the King's commands? Definitely NOT. There is no way to be a citizen of a nation (**YAHUAH**'s Nation) if one does not obey the laws established in that nation.

John 14: ⁶ *YAHUSHA said to him: I am the way, and the truth, and the life; no one comes to the Father (**YAHUAH**), but for me (**YAHUSHA**).*

For example, you are not considered a citizen of a nation if you do not celebrate and look forward to the independence day of your country. So how do you think you can be considered a citizen of the kingdom of **YAHUAH** if you do not celebrate the King's holidays and the independence of the Kingdom?

However, the HARDEST and BITTER thing is that these laws and holidays are not for everyone, but are ONLY for the children or citizens of the kingdom. The sons of perdition will never celebrate, nor will they be interested in the laws of the kingdom of **YAHUAH**, because they do not belong to the group of the elect. They already have another citizenship or king, that is, the citizenship of perdition: they obey the laws of the father of perdition.

This means that the content of this work is not for everyone. It is possible that the vast majority say that they are nonsense or that this is not what they have been taught since childhood. Perhaps they simply say that the concepts developed are lies and therefore try to justify their actions contrary to the truth. This is because they are not part of the chosen ones.

When your heart makes you understand and accept the truth, no matter how hard or difficult it may seem, you will know that you are part of the citizens of the kingdom. The badge that the citizens of the kingdom of **YAHUAH** wear is to recognize the commandments of **YAHUAH** in their life, to keep them and to see his feasts, actions that function as the seal that closes the covenant as a citizen of the kingdom.

Jubilees 2: [17-18]. *And he gave us a great sign, the Shabbath day, that we should work six days, but keep the Shabbath on the seventh day from all work. 18. And all the angels **of the presence**, and all the angels **of sanctification**, these two great kinds: He has hidden us to keep the Shabbath with Him in heaven and on earth.*

I share these two verses so that we can better

understand that it is not for everyone or for all of humanity, it is only for **YAHUAH**'s chosen ones. Some people think that all the angels keep the Shabbath and that all humanity recognizes and accepts the commandments of **YAHUAH**. However, this is far from the truth.

YAHUAH selected only two categories of angels to keep the Shabbath with Him: *To all the angels of the presence and to all the angels of sanctification.* That is, to the elect angels, those who are closest to **YAHUAH** and who are constantly in His presence and in Sanctification with Him. This privilege of keeping the Shabbath was not given to all angels, just as it was not given to all mankind. This is a privilege given solely and exclusively to the children or citizens of the kingdom of **YAHUAH**.

We can take the parable of the 10 virgins in Matthew 25 as an analogy: only the prudent were ready and waiting for their husbands. In the same way, only those who are watching, waiting and longing for the feasts of **YAHUAH** will be attentive and prepared for the coming of **YAHUSHA**. The badge is for those who are keeping His commandments (including the Shabbath as a Shabbath) and for those who are prepared by celebrating His feasts as an eternal reminder of His coming and His eternal redemption.

Are you a citizen of the kingdom of **YAHUAH**? Are you watching and observing the King's feasts?

Only you and no one else has the answer to these questions. Just make sure that it is not too late and that you are not caught in the nets of the adversary's excuses, those that only lead to eternal perdition. Make sure you are a citizen of the kingdom of **YAHUAH** through our eternal ambassador **YAHUSHA**.

Romans 10: [9] *That if you shall confess with your mouth **YAHUSHA** is your Master, and shall believe in your heart that **ELOHIYM** has raised him from the dead, you shall be saved.*

Sometimes we don't know what it's like to believe with our heart and not with our mind. This means that our whole being has the certainty or conviction that **YAHUSHA** is our Master and Mâshîyach. Our heart is the engine of our lives and that is why there is no room for doubt or for any strange thoughts.

If the heart (physical organ) stops for a few seconds, we die instantly. This means that our heart (not as a physical organ) is the perfect core for our conviction and belief in **YAHUSHA**. Any thought can persuade or dissuade the one who believes with the mind, however, never the one who believes with the heart.

In conclusion, whether you believe these words or not is not a regret for me. That you decide not to listen and justify yourself in every possible way is also none of my business. These words are only and exclusively for the children of the kingdom, for those citizens of **YAHUAH** who are still sleeping and who need to be awakened to be partakers of the new kingdom. This is not for everyone.

CONCLUSION

Through this study we have come across a lot of new and shocking information, everything is available to the public.

The main objective of this short guide is to provide each reader with the pertinent information to approach **YAHUAH**, to know His commandments and the Feasts of **YAHUAH** or the Biblical Feasts, so that we understand that they are still valid and that they are non-negotiable and much less replaceable by commandments of men or pagan holidays.

Perhaps some will wonder how we came to change His commandments and forget his Feasts even though they have always been present in the Bible. The answer is, as we have already said, that it all began with Constantine. So many things happened in history that not even several books would be enough to share the events that changed the world in such a drastic way to the point of taking humanity away from its Creator **YAHUAH**.

Remember that the mandate of Constantine and the leaders of the church was that there could not be, nor could they accept, any god other than the one created by the empire, much less any practice that did not follow the norms that they had created. This led to calling and branding people as heretics with a death sentence and persecution if:

● *Someone kept Saturday (Shabbath according to the Bible) as a Shabbath instead of Sunday (the day created by Constantine and his leaders)*

● *Someone kept or practiced the Biblical Feasts instead of the pagan holidays.*

● *Someone did not accept the new god of the empire and publicly declared to follow him.*

● *If someone was considered a Yahudiy or a Yâshârêl.*

These are just some points that stand out, since the religion and acceptance of the new god of the Roman Empire was MANDATORY, that is, it was OBLIGATORY to serve him, and the one who did not serve him became an enemy of the church and the state and, consequently, was a heretic sentenced to death.

Likewise, it was obligatory to accept the books that the empire had declared as valid or as an inspired word, and anyone who tried to translate or make the Bible available to the masses was worthy of the stake, excommunicated and persecuted...

All these practices led to the commandments (Fourth Commandment to Keep the Shabbath) and the feasts of **YAHUAH** they'd be forgotten and, instead of them, the new pagan holidays declared by the empire and its leaders will be practiced. In addition, the man-made commandment that establishes the substitution of Saturday for Sunday is kept.

In short, the goal has always been the same: to distance humanity from its Creator **YAHUAH** and drag him to the ruins and eternal perdition.

Romans 3: *2 For all have sinned, and come short of the glory of **YAHUAH**.*

Let us not forget that we were all born in sin and out of the glory of **YAHUAH**, so the enemy's goal is to keep us away from the knowledge of **YAHUAH** in order that we may not know the truth and not worship Him. This is because, if we come to know the truth, we will then serve **YAHUAH** and we will be reconciled through **YAHUSHA** with our Creator **YAHUAH**.

By keeping His commandments and remembering His holidays we are demonstrating our love for **YAHUAH**. **John 14**: *15If you love me, keep my commandments.* This tells us that there is only one way to show our love for Him and that is by keeping His commandments. This has nothing to do with feelings, what we feel or don't feel, much less the word. This has to do with action, that our actions demonstrate the love we have for our Creator **YAHUAH** and Salvador **YAHUSHA** by keeping His commandments. How do we know then that we love him? When we keep His commandments.

Matthew 21: *28 But what do you think? A man had two sons, and he went up to the first and said to him, "Son, go and work in my vineyard today." 29Responding he said: **I don't want to; but***

*afterwards, repenting, he went. ³⁰And coming up to the other, he said to him in the same way; and he answering, said: **Yes, sir, I'm coming. And he went not.** ³¹ Which of the two did his father's will? And they said, The first. **YAHUSHA** said unto them, Verily I say unto you, that the publicans and the harlots go before you into the kingdom of **ELOHIYM**.*

This is so that we understand that it is not of the one who says, but of the one who does; in other words, it is necessary to do. But to do what? Some would ask. To do the will of the Father (**YAHUAH**). And what is the will of the Father (**YAHUAH**)? That we keep His commandments.

So, if **YAHUAH** says that his commandments and his Feasts are PERPETUAL, that is, forever, for me they will always be, because not only it is what He said, but also perpetual means that it has no expiration limit.

Moreover, if we see **YAHUSHA, the disciples and apostles** celebrating all the feasts and following the commandments, do we have more authority than they to abolish them or modify the commandments? The answer is a simple NO.

Let us set the commandments and the Feasts of **YAHUAH** as priority events in our lives; they should be days of joy and enjoyment for all of us. In this way we will realize that we have been missing out on all the enjoyment that **YAHUAH ELOHIYM** has prepared for us. Remember, these are feasts of **YAHUAH**, as a reminder for us to enjoy, get out of the ritual and enjoy the feasts, so that our family and friends are eager for those holidays to come as it will be shared, tasted and enjoyed with **YAHUAH** in our lives.

Joshua 24: [15] *And if it seem evil unto you to serve* **YAHUAH**, *choose you this day whom you will serve; whether the Gods which your fathers served that were on the other side of the flood, or the Gods of the Ĕmôrîy, in whose land you dwell: but as for me and my house, we will serve* **YAHUAH**.

If we paraphrase the words of **YAHUSHA** in this verse, they say, *"And if it seems evil to you to serve* **YAHUAH**, *choose you today whom you will serve... But Me and My house will serve* **YAHUAH**" and we will celebrate the feasts of **YAHUAH**.

In conclusion, it is not my goal to change the thoughts or the way of being of any person. My main goal is to share the truth of the scriptures; then you will decide whether to believe it or not. If you find something in this guide that you don't like or that you disagree with, I recommend that you do your own research. The truth will certainly reach the children of light, because the children of darkness will never accept the truth as it is.

The children of darkness or of perdition will always seek to adorn the truth in such a way that it sounds like it is clothed with truth and credible when, in reality, it is full of lies. It is my continuous prayer that everyone who manages to read this guide can reach freedom and truth. **John 8**: [32] *and you will know the truth, and the truth will set you free.* I hope that one day they can become free in the truth that is in **YAHUSHA** our Savior.

PRAYER

My **YAHUAH ELOHIYM**, I am thankful for this opportunity to be able to share Your Word and Your truth. Thank you for giving me the opportunity to restore real name in the bible and in this guide.

I beg you to touch the readers and bring them to the knowledge of Your name. I pray that Your feasts will start to become a part of our lives.

Bless, protect, give understanding and wisdom to the reader leading him to the knowledge of Your only truth, in the powerful name of Your beloved Son **YAHUSHA**. Amen.

BIOGRAPHY

Yeral E. Ogando comes from a very humble origin and continues to be a humble servant of our Almighty Savior YAHUSHA; understanding that we are nothing but vessels and the YAHUAH calls us and sends us also to do His work, not our work.

Luke 17:10 *"So you also, when you have done all that has been commanded you, say: We are useless servants, for what we should have done, we did"*.

Dr. Ogando was born in the Caribbean, Dominican Republic. He is the beloved father of five beautiful children, two girls, Yeiris and Tiffany and three boys, Bennett, Ethan and Nathan.

YAHUSHA brought Him to His feet at the age of 16-17 years. Since then, he has served as a Co-pastor,

Pastor, Bible teacher in schools, youth counselor, planter and church founder.

Fluent in several languages, Dr. Ogando is the Creator and owner of an Online Translation Ministry that has been operating since 2007; with Native Christian translators in more than 25 countries.

(www.christian-translation.com),

The most exciting thing about his Translation Ministry is that thousands of people are receiving the Word of YAHUAH in their native language daily and hundreds of ministries manage to reach the world through the work of Christian-translation.com together with its network of translators in more than 25 countries to more than 375 languages.

BIBLIOGRAPHY

● J. (2020, September 23). Wikipedia. https://es.wikipedia.org/wiki/J

● MINEDUC. (n.f.). www.mineduc.gob.gt . Retrieved on April 30, 2022, from https://www.mineduc.gob.gt/DIGECADE/documents/Telesecundaria/Recursos%20Digitales/2o%20Recursos%20Digitales%20TS%20BY-SA%203.0/03%20COMUNICACION%20Y%20LENGUAJE/U1%20pp%2023%20uso%20v.pdf

● The name of ELOHIYM in Swahili: how he became known. (n.f.). JW.ORG . Retrieved on April 30, 2022, from https://www.jw.org/es/biblioteca/revistas/wp20120901/nombre-de-dios-en-suajili/

● Oh, ELOHIYM. (n.f.). Etymologies of Chile - Dictionary That Explains the Origin of Words. http://etimologias.dechile.net/?Dios

● Zeus. (2021, July 22). Wikipedia. https://es.wikipedia.org/wiki/Zeus

● Jesus (name). (2005, August 9). male name. Wikipedia. https://es.wikipedia.org/wiki/ Jes%C3%BAs_ (name)

● The editors of the Encyclopedia Britannica. (2018). Jupiter | Roman ELOHIYM In Encyclopedia Britannica. https://www.britannica. com/topic/Jupiter-Roman-ELOHIYM

● Book of Eskra caps 48-60; bk 28 of the standard edition of OAHSPE. (n.f.). Oahspestandardedition. com . Retrieved on April 30, 2022, from https:// oahspestandardedition.com/OSE_28f.html

● Ashkenazi. (2005, April 27). Yahudiyish community originating from eastern, northern, central and northwestern Europe. Wikipedia. https://es.wikipedia.org/wiki/Asquenaz%C3%AD

● Esus. (2021, June 27). Wikipedia. https:// es.wikipedia.org/wiki/Esus

● Book of Eskra caps 48-60; bk 28 of the standard edition of OAHSPE. (n.f.). Oahspestandardedition. com . https://oahspestandardedition.com/OSE_28f. html

● Septuagint. (2022, April 6). Wikipedia. https:// es.wikipedia.org/wiki/Septuaginta

● Vulgate. (2022, April 17). Wikipedia https:// es.wikipedia.org/wiki/Vulgata

● Alphonsine Bible. (2022, April 20). Wikipedia. https://es.wikipedia.org/wiki/Biblia_alfonsina

● Queen's Cassiodorus. A life on the run for translating the Bible into Spanish. (2019, August

22). Wake up to the new Editions. https://www.despertaferro-ediciones.com/2019/casiodoro-de-reina-traducir-la-biblia-al-castellano/

● The history of calendars. (2020, February 25). The Avant-garde. https://www.lavanguardia.com/vida/junior-report/20200224/473743933476/historia-calendarios-astronomia-tiempo-cultura.html

● Ra. (2003, August). Deity of ancient Mitsrayim. Wikipedia. https://es.wikipedia.org/wiki/Ra_(mytholog%C3%ADa)

● Origin of the Calendar - Types and Evolution. (2021, September 7). Curiosphere History. https://curiosfera-historia.com/historia-del-calendario/

● Univision. (n.f.). 5 types of calendars that are used in different parts of the world. Univision. Retrieved on April 30, 2022, from https://www.univision.com/explora/5-tipos-de-calendarios-que-se-utilizan-en-diferentes-partes-del-mundo

● The Julian calendar. (2022, April 4). Wikipedia. https://es.wikipedia.org/wiki/Calendario_juliano

● Contributors to the Wikimedia projects. (2004, July 15). The Roman ELOHIYM of war. Wikipedia. https://es.wikipedia.org/wiki/Marte_(mytholog%C3%ADa)

● Romulus and Remus. (2003, October 14).The legendary founders of Rome. Wikipedia. https://es.wikipedia.org/wiki/R%C3%B3mulo_y_Remo

● Bona Dea. (2021, October 23). Wikipedia.

https://es.wikipedia.org/wiki/Bona_Dea

● Juno. (mythology). (May 9, 2006). Juno (mythology). Wikipedia. https://es.wikipedia.org/wiki/Juno_ (mytholog%C3%ADa)

● Jano. (2022, February 27). Wikipedia. https://oo.wikipedia.org/wiki/Jano

● February. (2019, December 16). Wikipedia. https://es.wikipedia.org/wiki/Februa

● Julius Caesar. (n.f.). Wikipedia. https://es.wikipedia.org/wiki/Julio_C%C3%A9sar

● Octavius Augustus. (2022, April 21). Wikipedia. https://es.wikipedia.org/wiki/Octavio_Augusto

● December 25th. (2021, December 20). Stories And Stories In Mexico. https://relatosehistorias.mx/nuestras-historias/25-de-diciembre

● The Gregorian calendar. (2022, April 8). Wikipedia. https://es.wikipedia.org/wiki/Calendario_gregoriano

● Definition of alba — Definition of. (n.f.). Retrieved on April 30, 2022, from https://definicion.de/alba/

● ASALE, R.-, & RAE. (n.f.). perpetuo, perpetuo "Diccionario de La Lengua Española" - Tercentenary Edition. https://dle.rae.es/perpetuo

● ASALE, R.-, & RAE. (n.f.). Idol, idol "Dictionary of the Spanish Language" - Tercentenary Edition. https://dle.rae.es/%C3%ADdolo

www.ingramcontent.com/pod-product-compliance
Lightning Source LLC
La Vergne TN
LVHW051735080426
835511LV00018B/3077